PENGUIN BOOKS
GERMAN PHRASE BOOK

D1022901

OTHER PENGUIN PHRASE BOOKS
French
Italian
Portuguese
Spanish

GERMAN
PHRASE BOOK

THIRD EDITION

JILL NORMAN

UTE HITCHIN

PENGUIN BOOKS

PENGUIN BOOKS

Published by the Penguin Group
27 Wrights Lane, London W8 5TZ, England
Viking Penguin Inc., 40 West 23rd Street, New York, New York 10010, USA
Penguin Books Australia Ltd, Ringwood, Victoria, Australia
Penguin Books Canada Ltd, 2801 John Street, Markham, Ontario, Canada L3R 1B4
Penguin Books (NZ) Ltd, 182–190 Wairau Road, Auckland 10, New Zealand

Penguin Books Ltd, Registered Offices: Harmondsworth, Middlesex, England

First published in 1968
Second edition 1978
Third edition 1988
5 7 9 10 8 6 4

Copyright © Jill Norman and Ute Hitchin, 1968, 1978, 1988
All rights reserved

Made and printed in Great Britain by
Richard Clay Ltd, Bungay, Suffolk
Filmset in Linotron 202 Ehrhardt by
Morton Word Processing, Scarborough

CONTENTS

SHOPPING & SERVICES ▪ 111

POST OFFICE ▪ 142

SIGHTSEEING ▪ 147

ENTERTAINMENT ▪ 154

SPORTS AND GAMES ▪ 157

INTRODUCTION

In this series of phrase books only those words and phrases that might be called essential to a traveller have been included, but the definition of 'traveller' has been made very wide, to include not only the business traveller and the holiday-maker, whether travelling alone, with a group or the family, but also the person who rents or owns a house or an apartment. Each type of traveller has his or her own requirements, and for easy use the phrases are arranged in sections which deal with specific situations.

Pronunciation is given for each phrase and for all words in the extensive vocabulary. An explanation of the system used for the pronunciation guide is to be found on pages xi–xiii. It is essential to read this section carefully before starting to use this book.

Some of the German phrases are marked with an asterisk*– these attempt to give an indication of the kind of reply you might get to your question, and of questions you may be asked in your turn.

For those who would like to know a little more about the German language, a brief survey of the main points of its grammar is provided at the end of the book (pages 206–22).

PRONUNCIATION

The pronunciation guide is intended for people with no knowledge of German. As far as possible the system is based on English pronunciation. This means that complete accuracy may sometimes be lost for the sake of simplicity, but the reader should be able to understand German pronunciation, and make himself understood, if he reads this section carefully. In addition, each phrase and word is given with a pronunciation guide. Stressed syllables are printed in **bold type**.

VOWELS

German vowels are much purer than English.

Long a	as 'a' in father	symbol ah	Abend – ahbent
Short a	as 'a' in allow	symbol a	Wald – valt
au	as 'ow' in how	symbol ow	Ausland – owslant
ä	as 'a' in late or 'e' in bed	symbol e or ai/ay	Gepäck – gepeck; spät – shpayt
äu	as 'oy' in boy	symbol oy	Gebäude – geboyder
Long e	as 'e' in they	symbol ay	gegen – gaygen
Short e	as 'e' in bed	symbol e	Bett – bet

e (final)	unlike English 'e' is pronounced at the end of a word, as 'er' in sister	symbol er	Tinte – tinter
	(NB 'er': in most cases the r is more pronounced than in English)	symbol air/er	Vater – fahtair Amerika – amaireekah
eu	as 'oy' in boy	symbol oy	Feuer – foyer
ei	as 'i' in fine	symbol ī	ein-īn leisten – līsten
i	as 'i' in bit	symbol i	Schiff – shif
i	as 'ee' in weed	symbol ee	Familie – fameelyer
ie	as 'ee' in meet	symbol ee	Bier – beer
Long o	as 'o' in nose	symbol oh	sofort – zohfort
Short o	as 'o' in not	symbol o	von – fon
ö	similar to sound in 'her' and 'first' but made with the lips well rounded	symbol er	schön – shern
u	as 'oo' in good	symbol oo	Blut – bloot
ü	similar to some Scottish pronunciations of 'u'. Say 'i' as in bit with the lips rounded and pushed forward	symbol ui	Büro – buiroh

CONSONANTS

b (final)	and before a consonant, pronounced as 'p'		ab – ap

ch	rather like the sound of 'ch' in Scottish loch or the Welsh 'ch'	symbol kh	Buch – bookh
chs	as 'x' in six	symbol x or ks	Lachs – luks
d (final)	pronounced as 't'		Kind – kint
g	hard as 'g' in go, except in some endings		gut – goot
j	as 'y' in you	symbol y	ja – yah
kn	in German words which begin k-n the two sounds are pronounced separately, unlike English	symbol k-n	Knie – k-nee
qu	two sounds pronounced separately	symbol kv	Qualität – kvalitayt
r	is always guttural and clearly pronounced		
s	before a vowel is pronounced 'z' as in zoo	symbol z	Bluse – bloozer
s	at the end of a word is pronounced 's' as in sale	symbol s/ss	Hals – hals das – dass
s	before p or t is pronounced 'sh' as in sheep	symbol sh	Stein – shtīne Spiel – shpeel
sch	as 'sh' in sheep	symbol sh	Schuh – shoo
ss	sometimes printed ß in German and pronounced as in English		
th	as 't' in tent	symbol t	Theater – tayahtair
tz	as 'ts' in cuts	symbol ts	Netz – nets
v	as 'f' in foot or 'v' in vase	symbol f or v	viel – feel;
w	usually as 'v' in vase	symbol v	Wohnung – vohnoon
x	as 'x' in wax	symbol x or ks	Taxi – taksee
z	as 'ts' in bits	symbol ts	zu – tsoo

ESSENTIALS

FIRST THINGS

Yes	**Ja**	**Yah**
No	**Nein**	**Nīn**
Please	**Bitte**	**Bitter**
Thank you	**Danke**	**Danker**
You're welcome	**Bitte sehr**	**Bitter** zayr

LANGUAGE PROBLEMS

| I'm English/American | **Ich bin Engländer(in)/ Amerikaner(in)** | Ikh bin **englender(in)/ amaireekahnair(in)** |
| Do you speak English? | **Sprechen Sie Englisch?** | **Shprekhen** zee **english** |

Does anybody here speak English?	Spricht hier irgend jemand Englisch?	Shprikht heer eergent yaymant english
I don't speak (much) German	Ich spreche kein/nur wenig Deutsch	Ikh shprekher kīn/noor vainikh doytsh
Do you understand (me)?	*Verstehen Sie (mich)?	Fairshtayen zee mikh
I (don't) understand	Ich verstehe (nicht)	Ikh fairshtayer nikht
Would you say that again, please?	Würden Sie das bitte noch einmal sagen?	Vuirden zee das bitter nokh īnmal zahgen
Please speak slowly	Bitte, sprechen Sie langsam	Bitter shprekhen zee langzam
What does that mean?	Was bedeutet das?	Vas bedoytet das
Can you translate this for me?	Können Sie das für mich übersetzen?	Kernen zee das fuir mikh uiber-zetsen
Please write it down	Bitte schreiben Sie es auf	Bitter shrīben zee es owf
What do you call this in German?	Wie heisst das auf Deutsch?	Vee hīst das owf doytsh
How do you say that in German?	Wie sagt man das auf Deutsch?	Vee zakht man das owf doytsh
Please show me the word in the book	Bitte zeigen Sie mir das Wort im Buch	Bitter tsīgen zee meer das vort im bookh

QUESTIONS

Where is/are ...?	**Wo ist/sind ...?**	Voh ist/zint
When?	**Wann?**	Van
How?	**Wie?**	Vee
How much is/are ...?	**Wie teuer ist/sind ...?/Was kostet/kosten ...?**	Vee toyer ist/zint/vas kostet/kosten
How much/many?	**Wie viel/viele?**	Vee feel/feeler
How long?	**Wie lange?**	Vee langer
How far?	**Wie weit?**	Vee vīt
What's that?	**Was ist das?**	Vas ist das
Who is that?	**Wer ist das?**	Vair ist das
What do you want?	**Was wünschen Sie?**	Vas vuinshen zee
What must I do?	**Was muss ich tun?**	Vas moos ikh toon
Why?	**Warum?**	Vahroom
Have you ...?	**Haben Sie ...?**	Hahben zee
Is there ...?	**Gibt es ...?**	Geept es
Have you seen ...?	**Haben Sie ... gesehen?**	Hahben zee ... gezayen
Where can I find?	**Wo kann ich ... finden?**	Voh kan ikh ... finden
May I have ...?	**Darf ich ... haben?**	Darf ikh ... hahben
What is the matter?	**Was ist los?**	Vas ist los
Can I help you?	***Kann ich Ihnen helfen?**	Kan ikh eenen helfen

Can you help me?	**Können Sie mir helfen?**	Kernen zee meer helfen
Can you tell/give/show me?	**Können Sie mir ... sagen/geben/zeigen?**	Kernen zee meer ... zahgen/gayben/tsīgen

USEFUL STATEMENTS

It is ...	**Es ist ...**	Es ist
It isn't ...	**Es ist nicht ...**	Es ist nikht
I have ...	**Ich habe ...**	Ikh hahber
I don't have ...	**Ich habe nicht ...**	Ikh hahber nikht
I want ...	**Ich will ...**	Ikh vill
I would like ...	**Ich möchte ...**	Ikh merkhter
I need ...	**Ich brauche ...**	Ikh browkher
I like it	**Es gefällt mir**	Es gefellt meer
OK/that's fine	**OK/das ist gut so**	Das ist goot zoh
Here is/are ...	**Hier ist/sind ...**	Heer ist/zint
I (don't) like it	**Es gefällt mir (nicht)**	Es gefellt meer (nikht)
I (don't) know	**Ich weiss (nicht)**	Ikh vīs (nikht)
I didn't know that ...	**Ich wusste nicht, dass ...**	Ikh vooster nikht das
I think so	**Ich glaube**	Ikh glowber
I'm hungry/thirsty	**Ich habe Hunger/Durst**	Ikh hahber hoonger/doorst
I'm tired/ready	**Ich bin müde/fertig**	Ikh bin muider/fairtikh

Leave me alone	Lassen Sie mich in Ruhe	Lassen zee mikh in **rooer**
I'm lost	Ich habe mich verlaufen	Ikh **hah**ber mikh fair**low**fen
We're looking for ...	Wir suchen ...	Veer **zook**hen
Here it is	Hier ist es	Heer ist es
There they are	Dort sind sie	Dort zint zee
There is/are ...	Es gibt ...	Es geept
It's important	Es ist wichtig	Es ist **vikh**tikh
It's urgent	Es ist dringend	Es ist **dring**ent
You are mistaken	Sie irren sich	Zee **irr**en zikh
Just a minute	Einen Augenblick	**In**en **owg**enblik
This way, please	Hier entlang bitte	Heer entlang **bitt**er
Take a seat	Nehmen Sie Platz	**Nay**men zee plats
Come in!	Herein!	Her-**in**
It's cheap	Es ist billig	Es ist **bill**ikh
It's (too) expensive	Es ist (zu) teuer	Es ist (tsoo) **toy**er
That's all	Das ist alles	Das ist **all**es
You're right	Sie haben recht	Zee **hah**ben rekht
You're wrong	Das stimmt nicht	Das shtimt nikht

GREETINGS

Good morning	Guten Morgen	**Goo**ten **mor**gen
Good day/afternoon	Guten Tag	**Goo**ten **tahg**
Good evening	Guten Abend	**Goo**ten **ah**bent

Good night	**Gute Nacht**	**Goo**ter nakht
Goodbye	**Auf Wiedersehen**	Auf veedair-zayn
How are you?	**Wie geht es Ihnen?**	Vee gayt es **ee**nen
Very well, thank you	**Danke, gut**	**dan**ker goot
See you soon/ tomorrow	**Bis bald/morgen**	bis balt/**mor**gen
Have a good journey	**Gute Reise**	**Goo**ter **rī**zer
Have a good time	**Viel Vergnügen**	Feel fairg-**nui**gen
Good luck/all the best	**Viel Glück/alles Gute**	Feel gluick/**al**les **goo**ter

POLITE PHRASES

Sorry	**Verzeihung**	Fer-**tsī**-oong
Excuse me	**Entschuldigen Sie bitte**	Ent**shool**digen zee **bit**ter
Is everything all right?	**Alles in Ordnung?**	**Al**les in **ord**noong
Don't mention it/ you're welcome	**Bitte sehr**	**Bit**ter zayr
Don't worry	**Machen Sie sich keine Sorgen**	**Mak**hen zee zikh **kī**ner **zor**gen
With pleasure	**Mit Vergnügen**	Mit fairg-**nui**gen
It's a pity	**(Es ist) schade**	Es ist **shah**der
It doesn't matter	**(Es) macht nichts**	Es makht **nikh**ts
I beg your pardon?	**Wie bitte?**	Vee **bit**ter
Am I disturbing you?	**Störe ich Sie?**	**Ster**er ikh zee

I'm sorry to have troubled you	Es tut mir leid, dass ich Sie belästigt habe	Es toot meer līt das ikh zee belestigt hahber
Good/that's fine	Gut/das ist gut so	Goot/das ist goot zoh
Thanks for your trouble	Besten Dank für Ihre Mühe	Besten dank fuir eerer mui-er

OPPOSITES

before/after	vor/nach	for/nakh
early/late	früh/spät	frui/shpayt
first/last	erste/letzte	airster/letster
now/later, then	jetzt/dann	yetst/dan
far/near	weit/nah	vīt/nah
here/there	hier/dort	heer/dort
in/out	in/aus	in/ows
inside/outside	drinnen/draussen	drinnen/drowsen
under/over	unter/über	oontair/uibair
big, large/small	gross/klein	grohs/klīne
deep/shallow	tief/seicht	teef/zīkht
empty/full	leer/voll	layr/fol
fat/lean	fett, dick/mager	fet, dick/mahgair
heavy/light	schwer/leicht	shvair/līkht
high/low	hoch/niedrig	hokh/needrikh
long, tall/short	lang/kurz	lang/koorts

narrow/wide	schmal/breit	shmahl/brīt
thick/thin	dick/dünn	dick/duin
least/most	mindest/meist	mindest/mīst
many/few	viel(e)/wenig(e)	feel/vaynikh
more/less	mehr/weniger	mair/vaynigair
much/little	viel/wenig	feel/vaynikh
beautiful/ugly	schön/hässlich	shern/heslikh
better/worse	besser/schlechter	besser/shlekhter
cheap/expensive	billig/teuer	billikh/toyer
clean/dirty	sauber/schmutzig	zowber/shmootsikh
cold/hot, warm	kalt/heiss, warm	kalt/hīs, varm
easy/difficult	leicht/schwierig	līkht/shveerikh
fresh/stale	frisch/schal, alt	frish/shahl, alt
good/bad	gut/schlecht	goot/shlekht
new, young/old	neu, jung/alt	noy, yoong/alt
nice/nasty	nett/eklig	net/ayklikh
right/wrong	richtig/falsch	reekhtikh/falsh
open/closed, shut	offen/geschlossen	offen/geshlossen
vacant/occupied	frei/besetzt	frī/bezetst
quick/slow	schnell/langsam	shnel/langzam
quiet/noisy	ruhig/laut	roo-ikh/lowt
sharp/blunt	scharf/stumpf	sharf/shtoompf

SIGNS & PUBLIC NOTICES[1]

Achtung	Caution
Aufzug	Lift/elevator
Ausgang	Exit
Auskunft	Information
Ausverkauf	Sale
Ausverkauft	Sold out/house full
Bank	Bank
Baustelle	Building site
Berühren verboten	Do not touch
Besetzt	Occupied/engaged
Betreten verboten	No trespassing
Betriebsferien	Public holidays
Bitte klingeln/klopfen	Please ring/knock
Damen	Ladies

1. See also ROAD SIGNS (p.41)

Dolmetscher	Interpreter
Drücken	Push
Einbahnstrasse	One way street
Eingang	Entrance
Eintritt frei	Admission free
Es wird gebeten, nicht ...	You are requested not to ...
Fernsprecher	Telephone
Feuermelder	Fire alarm
Frauen	Women
Frei	Free/vacant
(Fremden) führer	Guide
Fundbüro	Lost property office
Fussgänger	Pedestrians
Gefahr	Danger
Geöffnet von ... bis ...	Open from ... to ...
Geschlossen	Closed
Herren	Gentlemen
Kasse	Cash desk
Kein Eingang	No entry
Kein Trinkwasser	Not for drinking
Keine Zimmer frei	No vacancies
Kein Zutritt	No entry
Männer	Men
Nicht ...	Do not ...
Nichtraucher	No smoking
Notausgang	Emergency exit

Offen	Open
Polizei	Police
Post	Post office
Privat	Private
Rauchen verboten	No smoking
Rechts halten	Keep right
Reserviert	Reserved
Schlussverkauf	Sale
Selbstbedienung	Self service
Stehplätze	Standing room
Toilette	Lavatory/toilet
Trinkwasser	Drinking water
Unbefugten ist das Betreten verboten	Trespassers will be prosecuted
Vorsicht	Caution
Warten	Wait
Ziehen	Pull
Zimmer frei	Vacancies
Zimmer zu vermieten	Room to let
Zoll	Customs
Zutritt verboten	No admission

ABBREVIATIONS

ADAC	Allgemeiner Deutscher Automobil-Club	German Automobile Association

AG	**Aktien-Gesellschaft**	company
Bhf	**Bahnhof**	railway station
BRD	**Bundesrepublik Deutschland**	German Federal Republic
b.w.	**bitte wenden**	p.t.o.
DB	**Deutsche Bundesbahn**	German Railways
DDR	**Deutsche Demokratische Republik**	German Democratic Republic
d.h.	**das heisst**	i.e.
DIN	**Deutsche Industrie-Norm**	industrial standard (like B.S.)
DM	**Deutschmark**	German Mark
DSG	**Deutsche Schlafwagen-Gesellschaft**	German Sleeping Car Co.
EWG	**Europäische Wirtschafts-Gemeinschaft**	EEC
Frl.	**Fräulein**	Miss
GmbH	**Gesellschaft mit beschränkter Haftung**	limited company
Hbf.	**Hauptbahnhof**	central (main) station
km	**Kilometer**	kilometer (8 km = 5 miles)
Lkw	**Lastkraftwagen**	lorry, truck
m	**Meter**	metre
MEZ	**Mitteleuropäische Zeit**	Central European time
Min	**Minute**	minute

MWSt	**Mehrwehrtsteuer**	VAT
nachm.	**nachmittags**	in the afternoon
n.Chr.	**nach Christus**	AD
ÖAMTC	**Oesterreichischer Automobil- Motorrad- und Touring-Club**	Austrian Automobile, Motorcycle and Touring Club
ÖBB	**Oesterreichische Bundesbahnen**	Austrian Federal Railways
OO		toilet
Pf.	**Pfennig**	penny
Pkw	**Personenkraftwagen**	(private) car
Pl.	**Platz**	square
S-Bahn	**Vorortsbahn**	suburban line
SB	**Selbstbedienung**	self service
SBB	**Schweizerische Bundesbahnen**	Swiss Federal Railways
St.	**Stock**	floor
Std.	**Stunde**	hour
Str.	**Strasse**	street
tägl.	**täglich**	daily
TCS	**Touring-Club der Schweiz**	Swiss Touring Club
U-Bahn	**Untergrundbahn**	underground
usw.	**undsoweiter**	etc.
v.Chr.	**vor Christus**	BC
vorm.	**vormittags**	in the morning

WEZ	**Westeuropäische Zeit**	West European (Greenwich) time
z.B.	**zum Beispiel**	e.g.
z.Z.	**zur Zeit**	at present

MONEY[1]

Is there a bank that changes money near here?	**Gibt es eine Bank/ Wechselstube hier in der Nähe?**	Geept es īner bank/ veksel-shtoober heer in dair nayer
Do you cash travellers' cheques?	**Lösen Sie Reiseschecks ein?**	Lerzen zee rīze-sheks īn
Where can I cash travellers' cheques?	**Wo kann ich Reiseschecks einlösen?**	Voh kan ikh rīze-sheks īn-lerzen
I want to change some English/American money	**Ich möchte englisches/ amerikanisches Geld einwechseln**	Ikh merkhter englishes/ amaireekahnishes gelt īn-vekseln

1. In Germany banks are open Monday to Thursday 9 a.m. to 5 p.m., Friday 9 a.m. to 4 p.m., closed Saturday.
   In Austria banks are open from 8 a.m. to 12.30 p.m. and from 2.30 p.m. to 4 p.m., closed all day Saturday.
   In Switzerland they are open from 8 or 8.30 a.m. to 5 p.m., closed all day Saturday.

How much do I get for a pound/dollar?	Wieviel bekomme ich für ein englisches Pfund/einen Dollar?	Veefeel bekommer ikh fuir īn englishes pfoont/īnen dollar
Can you give me some small change?	Können Sie mir etwas Kleingeld geben?	Kernen zee meer etvas klīn-gelt gayben
Will you take a personal cheque/a credit card?	Nehmen Sie einen Barscheck/eine Kreditkarte?	Naymen zee īnen bahr-shek/īner kraydeet-karter
Do you have identification?	*Können Sie sich ausweisen?	Kernen zee zikh ows-vīzen
Do you have a cheque card?	*Haben Sie eine Euroscheckkarte?	Hahben zee īner oyrohshek-karter
Sign here, please	*Unterschreiben Sie hier bitte	Oonter-shrīben zee heer bitter
Where do I sign?	Wo muss ich unterschreiben?	Voh moos ikh oontair-shrīben
Go to the cashier	*Gehen Sie zur Kasse	Gayen zee tsoor kasser
What is the rate of exchange?	Wie ist der Wechselkurs?	Vee ist dair veksel-koors
I arranged for money to be transferred from England, has it arrived yet?	Ich habe veranlasst, dass Geld aus England überwiesen wird; ist es schon angekommen?	Ikh hahber fairanlast das gelt ows englant uibair-veezen veert ist es shohn angekommen
I want to open a bank account	Ich möchte ein Konto eröffnen	Ikh merkhter īn kontoh airerfnen

Please credit this to my account	**Bitte schreiben Sie das meinem Konto gut**	Bitter shrīben zee das mīnem kontoh goot
I'd like to get some cash with my credit card	**Ich möchte mit meiner Kreditkarte Bargeld einlösen**	Ikh merkhter mit mīnair kraydeet-karter bahrgelt īn-lerzen
Current account	**Das Girokonto**	Jeerohkontoh
Deposit account	**Das Sparkonto**	Shpahrkontoh
Statement	**Der Kontoauszug**	Kontoh-owstsoog
Balance	**Der Kontostand**	Kontoh-shtant
Cheque book	**Das Scheckbuch**	Shekbookh
Cheque card	**Die Scheckkarte**	Shek-karter

CURRENCY

Austria:	**100 Gr(oschen)**	= 1 S(chilling)
Germany:	**100 Pf(ennige)**	= 1 DM (Deutschmark)
Switzerland:	**100 c(entimes)**	= 1 F(ranc)

TRAVEL

ARRIVAL

PASSPORT CONTROL

Your passport, please	*Ihren Pass bitte	Eeren pass bitter
Are you together?	*Sind Sie zusammen?	Zint zee tsoozammen
I'm travelling alone	Ich reise allein	Ikh rīzer allīn
I'm travelling with my wife/a friend	Ich reise mit meiner Frau/einem Freund	Ikh rīzer mit mīnair frow/īnem froynt
I'm here on business/ on holiday	Ich bin geschäftlich/auf Urlaub hier	Ikh bin gesheftlikh/owf oorlowb heer
What is your address in …?	*Wie ist Ihre Adresse in …?	Vee ist eerer addresser in

| How long are you staying here? | ***Wie lange bleiben Sie hier?** | Vee **lang**er bl**ī**ben zee heer |

CUSTOMS

Nothing to declare	**Zollfreie Waren**	Tsoll-**frī**er vahren
Goods to declare	***Zollpflichtige Waren**	Tsoll-**pflikh**tiger **vah**ren
Which is your luggage?	***Welches ist Ihr Gepäck?**	Velkhes ist eer ge**peck**
Do you have any more luggage?	***Haben Sie noch mehr Gepäck?**	**Hah**ben zee nokh mayr ge**peck**
This is (all) my luggage	**Das ist (all) mein Gepäck**	Das ist (all) mīn ge**peck**
Have you anything to declare?	***Haben Sie etwas zu verzollen?**	**Hah**ben zee etvas tsoo fair**tsoll**en
I have only my personal things in it	**Ich habe nur persönliche Sachen darin**	Ikh **hah**ber noor pairzern**likh**er **zah**khen **dah**rin
I have a carton of cigarettes and a bottle of gin/wine	**Ich habe eine Stange Zigaretten und eine Flasche Gin/Wein**	Ikh **hah**ber **ī**ner **shtang**er tseega**rett**en oont **ī**ner **flash**er gin/vīn
You will have to pay duty on this	***Hierfür müssen Sie Zoll zahlen**	**Heer**fuir **muiss**en zee tsoll **tsah**len
Open your bag, please	***Öffnen Sie Ihre Tasche bitte**	**Erf**nen zee eerer tasher bitter
May I go through?	**Kann ich durchgehen?**	Kan ikh **doorkh**-gayen

LUGGAGE

My luggage has not arrived	Mein Gepäck ist noch nicht angekommen	Mīne gepeck ist nokh nikht angekommen
My luggage is damaged	Mein Gepäck ist beschädigt	Mīn gepeck ist beshaydikht
One suitcase is missing	Ein Koffer fehlt	Īn koffair faylt
Are there any luggage trolleys?	Gibt es hier Kofferkulis?	Geept es heer koffairkoolees
Where is the left luggage office?	Wo ist die Gepäckaufbewahrung?	Voh ist dee gepeckowfbevahroong
Luggage lockers	Das Schliessfach	Das shleesfakh

MOVING ON

Porter!	Gepäckträger!	Gepeck-traigair
Would you take these bags to a taxi/the bus	Bringen Sie bitte diese Taschen zu einem Taxi/zum Bus	Bringen zee bitter deezer tashen tsoo īnem taksee/tsoom boos
What is the price for each piece of luggage?	Wieviel verlangen Sie für jedes Gepäckstück?	Veefeel fairlangen zee fuir yaydes gepeck-shtuik
I shall take this myself	Ich nehme dies selbst	Ikh naymer dees zelbst
That's not mine	Das gehört mir nicht	Das gehert meer nikht
How much do I owe you?	Wieviel schulde ich Ihnen?	Veefeel shoolder ikh eenen

Where is the information bureau, please?	**Wo ist die Auskunft bitte?**	Voh ist dee **ows-koonft** bitter
Is there a bus/train into the town?	**Fährt ein Bus/Zug in die Stadt?**	Fairt in boos/tsoog in dee shtat
How can I get to ...?	**Wie komme ich nach ...?**	Vee kommer ikh nahkh ...

SIGNS TO LOOK FOR AT AIRPORTS AND STATIONS[1]

Arrivals	**Ankunft**
Booking office/tickets	**Fahrkarten(schalter)**
Buses	**Busse**
Car rental	**Autovermietung**
Connections	**Verbindungen**
Departures	**Abfahrt**
Exchange	**Wechselstube**
Gentlemen	**Herren/Männer**
Hotel reservations	**Zimmernachweis**
Information	**Auskunft**
Ladies' room	**Damen/Frauen**

1. Every German city has a **Verkehrsamt**. It gives information about entertainment and has a list of hotels and rooms, a **Hotel und Zimmernachweis**. It will recommend a hotel or guest-house, give you the price and the address, and direct you there. There is a small fee for this service.

Left luggage	Gepäckaufbewahrung
Lost property	Fundbüro
Luggage lockers	Schliessfächer
Main lines	Hauptstrecken
Newsstand	Zeitungsstand
Non-smoker	Nichtraucher
Platform	Gleis/Bahnsteig
Refreshments/Snack bar	Erfrischungen/Imbissstube
Reservations	Platzkarten
Smoker	Raucher
Suburban lines	S-Bahn/Vorortsbahn
Taxi rank	Taxistand
Tourist office	Fremdenverkehrsbüro
Transit desk	Transitschalter
Underground	U-Bahn
Waiting room	Warteraum

BUYING A TICKET

Where is the nearest travel agency?	Wo ist das nächste Reisebüro?	Voh ist das naikhster rīzer-buiroh
Have you a timetable, please?	Haben Sie einen Fahrplan bitte?	Hahben zee īnen fahrplahn bitter
What's the tourist return fare to …?	Wieviel kostet eine Touristen-Rückfahrkarte nach …?	Veefeel kostet īner tooristen-ruikfahr-karter nahkh

How much is it first class to ...?	Wieviel kostet es erster Klasse nach ...?	Veefeel kostet es airstair klasser nahkh
A second class single to ...	Einmal zweiter Klasse nach ...	Inmahl tsvitair klasser nahkh
Single/one way	Einfach	Infakh
A day return to ...	Eine Tagesrückfahrkarte nach ...	Iner tahges-ruikfahr-karter nahkh
Is there a cheaper midweek/weekend fare?	Gibt es verbilligte Fahrten in der Woche/am Wochenende?	Geept es fairbillikhter fahrten in dair vokher/am vokhenender
When are you coming back?	*Wann kommen Sie zurück?	Van kommen zee tsooruik
Is there a cheaper day ticket?	Gibt es eine billigere Tageskarte?	Geept es iner billigerer tahgeskarter
Is there a special rate for children?	Gibt es für Kinder Ermässigung?	Geept es fuir kindair airmesigoong
How old is he/she?	*Wie alt ist er/sie?	Vee alt ist air/zee
How long is this ticket valid?	Wie lange ist diese Fahrkarte gültig?	Vee langer ist deezer fahr-karter guiltikh
A book of tickets, please	Ein Fahrscheinheft bitte	In fahr-shin-heft bitter
Can I use it on the bus/underground too?	Gilt sie auch für den Bus/die U-Bahn?	Gilt zee owkh fuir dayn boos/dee oo-bahn
Is there a supplementary charge?	Muss man Zuschlag bezahlen?	Moos man tsoo-shlahg betsahlen

BY TRAIN

RESERVATIONS AND INQUIRIES

Where's the railway station/main station?	Wo ist der Bahnhof/ Hauptbahnhof?	Voh ist dair **bahn-hohf/ howpt-bahn-hohf**
Where is the ticket office?	Wo ist der Fahrkartenschalter?	Voh ist dair **fahr-karten-shaltair**
Two seats on the train to ...	Ich möchte zwei Plätze reservieren für den Zug nach ...	Ikh merkhter tsvī pletser rayzairveeren fuir dayn tsoog nahkh
I want to reserve a sleeper	Ich möchte einen Schlafwagenplatz reservieren	Ikh merkhter īnen shlahf-vahgen-plats rayzairveeren
How much does a couchette cost?	Wieviel kostet ein Liegeplatz?	Veefeel kostet īn leeger-plats
I want to register this luggage through to ...	Ich möchte dieses Gepäck als Reisegepäck nach ... aufgeben	Ikh merkhter deezes gepeck als rīzer-gepeck nahkh ... owfgayben
Is it an express or a local train?	Ist es ein Schnellzug oder ein Personenzug?	Ist es īn shnelltsoog ohdair īn pairzohnen-tsoog
Is there an earlier/later train?	Wann fährt der Zug davor/danach?	Van fairt dair tsoog dahfohr/dahnahkh
Is there a restaurant car on the train?	Hat der Zug einen Speisewagen?	Hat dair tsoog īnen shpīzer-vahgen

I want	Ich möchte	Ikh merkhter
a window seat	einen Fensterplatz	īnen fenstair-plats
a corner seat	einen Eckplatz	īnen ekplats
a seat in a non-smoking compartment	einen Platz im Nichtraucher-Abteil	īnen plats im nikht-rowkhair aptīl
When is the next train to ...?	Wann fährt der nächste Zug nach ...?	Van fairt dair naikhster tsoog nahkh
I'd like to make a motorail reservation	Ich möchte eine Reservierung für den Autozug	Ikh merkhter īner rayzairveeroong fuir dayn owtohtsoog
Where is the motorail loading platform for ...?	Wo ist der Verladebahnhof für Autozüge nach ...?	Voh ist dair fairlahder-bahnhof fuir owtohtsuiger nahkh

CHANGING

Is there a through train to ...?	Fährt ein Zug durch nach ...?	Fairt īn tsoog doorkh nahkh
Do I have to change?	Muss ich umsteigen?	Moos ikh oom-shtīgen
Where do I change?	Wo muss ich umsteigen?	Voh moos ikh oom-shtīgen
When is there a connection to ...?	Wann habe ich Anschluss nach ...?	Van hahber ikh anshloos nahkh
Change at ... and take the local train	*Steigen Sie in ... in den Personenzug um	Shtīgen zee in ... in dayn pairzohnentzoog oom

DEPARTURE

When does the train leave?	**Wann fährt der Zug ab?**	Van fairt dair tsoog ap
Which platform does the train to ... leave from?	**Von welchem Bahnsteig fährt der Zug nach ... ab?**	Fon velkhem **bahn-shtīg** fairt dair tsoog nahkh ... ap
Is this the train for ...?	**Ist dies der Zug nach ...?**	Ist dees dair tsoog nahkh
Close the doors	*Türen schliessen	Tuiren shleessen
There will be a delay of ...	*Sie müssen mit einer Verspätung von ... rechnen	Zee muissen mit īner fairshpaytoong fon ... rekhnen

ARRIVAL

When does the train get to ...?	**Wann kommt der Zug in ... an?**	Van kommt dair tsoog in ... an
Does the train stop at ...?	**Hält der Zug auch in ...?**	Helt dair tsoog owkh in
How long do we stop here?	**Wie lange halten wir hier?**	Vee **langer halt**en veer heer
Is the train late?	**Hat der Zug Verspätung?**	Hat dair tsoog fairshpaytoong
When does the train from ... get in?	**Wann fährt der Zug von ... ein?**	Van fairt dair tsoog fon ... īn
At which platform?	**Auf welchem Bahnsteig?**	Owf velkhem **bahn-shtīg**

| The train from ... is now arriving on platform ... | *Der Zug von ... hat Einfahrt auf Gleis ... | Dair tsoog fon ... hat īnfahrt owf glīs |

ON THE TRAIN

We have reserved seats	Wir haben Plätze reserviert	Veer hahben pletser rezairveert
Is this seat free?	Ist dieser Platz frei?	Ist deezair plats frī
This seat is taken	Dieser Platz ist besetzt	Deezair plats ist bezetst
Your tickets please	*Ihre Fahrkarten bitte	Eerer fahr-karten bitter
Is this a smoking/ non-smoking compartment?	Ist dies Raucher/ Nichtraucher?	Ist dees rowkhair/ nikhtrowkhair
Dining car	Der Speisewagen	Shpīzer-vahgen
When is the buffet car open?	Wann ist der Speisewagen geöffnet?	Van ist dair shpīzer-vahgen ge-erfnet
Where is the sleeping car?	Wo ist der Schlafwagen?	Voh ist dair shlahf-vahgen
Which is my sleeper?	Wo ist mein Schlafplatz?	Voh ist mīn shlahfplats
The heating is too high/low	Die Heizung ist zu warm/nicht warm genug	Dee hīt-tsoong ist tsoo varm/nikht varm genookh
I can't open/close the window	Ich kann das Fenster nicht öffnen/ schliessen	Ikh kan das fenstair nikht erfnen/shleessen

| What station is this? | **Wie heisst dieser Ort?** | Vee hīsst deezair ort |
| How long do we stop here? | **Wie lange halten wir hier?** | Vee langer halten veer heer |

BY AIR

Where's the airline office?	**Wo ist das Flugbüro?**	Voh ist das **floog**-buiroh
I'd like to book two seats on the plane to ...	**Ich möchte zwei Plätze buchen für das Flugzeug nach ...**	Ikh **merkh**ter tsvī **pletser** **book**hen fuir das **floog**-tsoyg nahkh
Is there a flight to ...?	**Gibt es einen Flug nach ...?**	Geept es īnen floog nahkh
When does the plane leave/arrive?	**Wann startet/landet das Flugzeug?**	Van **shtart**et/**land**et das **floog**-tsoyg
What is the flight number?	**Wie ist die Flugnummer?**	Vee ist dee **floog**-noommair
When's the next plane?	**Wann fliegt die nächste Maschine?**	Van fleegt dee **naikh**ster **mah**sheener
Is there a coach to the airport/town?	**Fährt ein Bus zum Flughafen/in die Stadt?**	Fairt īn boos tsoom **floog**-hahfen/in dee shtat
When must I check in?	**Wann muss ich mich melden?**	Van moos ikh mikh **meld**en
Please cancel my reservation to ...	**Bitte machen Sie meine Flugreservierung nach ... rückgängig**	**Bitter makhen** zee **mīner** **floog**-rezairveeroong nahkh ... **ruik**-gengikh

I'd like to change my reservation	Ich möchte meine Flugreservierung umbestellen	Ikh merkhter mīner floog-rezairveeroong oom-beshtellen
I have an open ticket	Ich habe eine Flugkarte mit offenem Rückflug	Ikh hahber īner floogkarter mit offenem ruikfloog
Can I change my ticket?	Kann ich meine Flugkarte umtauschen?	Kan ikh mīner floogkarter oomtowshen
Will it cost more?	Muss ich dazubezahlen?	Moos ikh dahtsoo-betsahlen

BY BOAT

Is there a boat-/(car) ferry from here to …?	Fährt ein Schiff/eine (Auto) Fähre von hier nach …?	Fairt īn shif/īner (owtoh) fairer fon heer nahkh
How long does the boat take?	Wie lange dauert die Fahrt?	Vee langer dowairt dee fahrt
How often does the boat leave?	Wie oft fährt ein Schiff ab?	Vee oft fairt īn shif ap
Does the boat call at …?	Legt das Schiff in … an?	Laygt das shif in … an
When does the next boat leave?	Wann fährt das nächste Schiff ab?	Van fairt das naikhster shif ap
Can I book a single berth cabin?	Kann ich eine Einzelkabine buchen?	Kan ikh īner īntsel-kahbeener bookhen
How many berths are there in the cabin?	Wieviele Betten sind in der Kabine?	Veefeeler betten zint in dair kahbeener

When must we go on board?	**Wann müssen wir an Bord gehen?**	Van muissen veer an bort gayen
How do we get on to the deck?	**Wie kommen wir an Deck?**	Vee kommen veer an deck
When do we dock?	**Wann legen wir an?**	Van laygen veer an
How long do we stay in port?	**Wie lange bleiben wir im Hafen?**	Vee langer blīben veer im hahfen
Hovercraft	**Das Hovercraft**	Hovairkrahft
Hydrofoil	**Das Tragflügelboot**	Trahgfluigelboht
Lifebelt	**Der Rettungsgürtel**	Rettoongs-guirtel
Lifeboat	**Das Rettungsboot**	Rettoongs-boht

BY UNDERGROUND

Where is the nearest underground station?	**Wo ist die nächste U-Bahnstation?**	Voh ist dee naikhster oo-bahn-shtatsyohn
Which line goes to ...?	**Welche Linie fährt nach ...?**	Velkher leenyer fairt nahkh
Does this train go to ...?	**Fährt dieser Zug nach ...?**	Fairt deezair tsoog nahkh
Where do I change for ...?	**Wo muss ich nach ... umsteigen?**	Voh moos ikh nahkh ... oomshtīgen
Is the next station ...?	**Ist die nächste Station ...?**	Ist dee naikhster shtatsyohn
What station is this?	**Welche Station ist dies?**	Velkher shtatsyohn ist dees
Have you an underground map?	**Haben Sie einen U-Bahn Plan?**	Hahben zee īnen oo-bahn plahn

BY BUS OR COACH

Where's the bus station?	Wo ist der Omnibus-Bahnhof?	Voh ist dair omniboos bahnhohf
Bus stop	*Bushaltestelle	Booshalte-shteller
Request stop	*Bedarfshaltestelle	Bedahrfs-haltesteller
When does the coach leave?	Wann fährt der Bus ab?	Van fairt dair boos ap
When does the coach get to …?	Wann kommt der Bus in … an?	Van kommt dair boos in … an
What stops does it make?	Wo hält der Bus überall?	Voh helt dair boos uiberal
How long is the journey?	Wie lange dauert die Fahrt?	Vee langer dowairt dee fahrt
We want to take a coach tour round the sights	Wir möchten eine Stadtrundfahrt machen	Veer merkhten iner shtat-roontfahrt makhen
Is there a sightseeing tour?	Gibt est eine Stadtrundfahrt?	Geept es iner shtat-roontfahrt
What is the fare?	Was kostet es?	Vas kostet es
Does the bus/coach stop at our hotel?	Hält der Bus bei unserem Hotel?	Helt dair boos bī oonzerem hohtel
Is there an excursion to … tomorrow?	Fährt morgen ein Sonderbus nach …?	Fairt morgen īn zondair-boos nahkh
When's the next bus?	Wann fährt der nächste Bus?	Van fairt dair naikhster boos

How often do the buses run?	Wie oft fahren die Busse?	Vee oft fahren dee boosser
Has the last bus gone?	Ist der letzte Bus schon weg?	Ist dair letster boos shohn veg
Does this bus go to the town centre? to the beach? to the station?	Fährt dieser Bus in die Stadtmitte? zum Strand? zum Bahnhof?	Fairt deezer boos in dee shtat-mitter tsoom shtrant tsoom bahn-hohf
Do you go near ...?	Fahren Sie in die Nähe von ...?	Fahren zee in dee nayer fon
Where can I get a bus to ...?	Von wo fährt ein Bus nach ...?	Fon voh fairt īn boos nahkh
Which bus goes to ...?	Welcher Bus fährt nach ...?	Velkhair boos fairt nahkh
I want to go to ...	Ich möchte nach ... fahren	Ikh merkhter nahkh ... fahren
Is this the right stop for ...?	Hält hier der Bus nach ...?	Helt heer dair boos nahkh
Where do I get off?	Wo muss ich aussteigen?	Voh moos ikh ows-shtīgen
I want to get off at ...	Ich möchte bei ... aussteigen	Ikh merkhter bī ... owsshtīgen
The tram to ... stops over there	*Die Strassenbahn nach ... hält dort drüben	Dee shtrahssen-bahn nahkh ... helt dort druiben
You must take a number ...	*Sie müssen mit der ... fahren	Zee muissen mit dair ... fahren
You get off at the next stop	*Sie müssen an der nächsten Haltestelle aussteigen	Zee muissen an dair naikhsten halter-shteller ows-shtīgen

| The trams run every ten minutes/every hour | *Die Strassenbahnen fahren alle zehn Minuten/jede Stunde | Dee shtrahssen-bahnen fahren aller tsayn meenooten/yayder shtoonder |

BY TAXI

Please get me a taxi	Rufen Sie mir bitte ein Taxi	Roofen zee meer bitter īn taksee
Where can I find a taxi?	Wo kann ich ein Taxi bekommen?	Voh kan ikh īn taksee bekommen
Are you free?	Sind Sie frei?	Zint zee frī
Please take me to the Hamburg hotel/the station/this address	Bitte fahren Sie mich zum Hotel Hamburg/zum Bahnhof/zu dieser Adresse	Bitter fahren zee mikh tsoom hohtel hamboorg/tsoom bahnhof/tsoo deezer addresser
Turn right/left at the next corner	Biegen Sie rechts/links an der nächsten Ecke ab	Beegen zee rekhts/links an dair naikhsten ecker ap
Straight on	Geradeaus	Gayrahder-ows
Can you hurry, I'm late?	Können Sie sich bitte beeilen, ich habe mich verspätet	Kernen zee zikh bitter be-īlen ikh hahber mikh fershpaytet
Please wait for me here	Bitte warten Sie auf mich	Bitter vahrten zee owf mikh
Stop here	Halten Sie hier	Halten zee heer
Is it far?	Ist es weit?	Ist es vīt

How much do you charge by the hour/ for the day?	**Wieviel verlangen Sie pro Stunde/pro Tag?**	Veefeel fer**lang**en zee pro **shtoon**der/pro tahg
How much will you charge to take me to ...?	**Wieviel verlangen Sie für die Fahrt nach ...?**	Veefeel fer**lang**en zee fuir dee fahrt nahkh
How much is it?	**Wieviel muss ich zahlen?**	Veefeel moos ikh **tsah**len
That's too much	**Das ist zu viel**	Das ist tsoo feel

DIRECTIONS

Excuse me, could you tell me ...?	**Entschuldigen Sie bitte, können Sie mir sagen ...**	Ent-**shool**digen zee **bitter kern**en zee meer **zah**gen
Where is ...?	**Wo ist ...?**	Voh ist
How do I get to ...?	**Wie komme ich nach ...?**	Vee **komme** ikh nahkh
How far is it to ...?	**Wie weit ist es nach ...?**	Vee vīt ist es nahkh
How many kilometres?	**Wieviel Kilometer?**	Veefeel **keelo**mayter
How do we get on to the motorway to ...?	**Wie kommen wir auf die Autobahn nach ...?**	Vee **kommen** veer owf dee **owtoh**-bahn nahkh
Which is the best road to ...?	**Welches ist die beste Strasse nach ...?**	Velkhes ist dee **bester shtrahss**er nahkh
Is this the right road for ...?	**Ist dies die Strasse nach ...?**	Ist dees dee **shtrahss**er nahkh

Is there a scenic route to …?	Gibt es eine Grüne Strasse nach …?	Geept es īner gruiner shtrahsser nahkh
Where does this road lead to?	Wohin führt diese Strasse?	Voh-hin fuirt deezer shtrahsser
Is it a good road?	Ist die Strasse gut?	Ist dee shtrahsser goot
Is it a motorway?	Ist es eine Autobahn?	Ist es īner owtoh-bahn
Is there a toll?	Muss man Zoll zahlen?	Moos man tsoll tsahlen
Is the tunnel/pass open?	Ist der Tunnel/Pass geöffnet?	Ist dair toon-nel/pass ge-erfnet
Is the road to … clear?	Ist die Strasse nach … frei?	Ist dee shtrahsser nahkh … frī
How far is the next village/petrol station?	Wie weit ist es bis zum nächsten Dorf/zur nächsten Tankstelle?	Vee vīt ist es bis tsoom naikhsten dorf/tsoor naikhsten tankshteller
Is there any danger of snowdrifts?	Besteht Gefahr von Schneewehen?	Bestayt gefahr fon shnay-vay-en
Will we get to … by evening?	Werden wir bis zum Abend in … sein?	Vairden veer bis tsoom ahbent in … zīn
How long will it take by car? by bicycle? on foot?	Wie lange fährt man mit dem Auto? mit dem Fahrrad? geht man zu Fuss?	Vee langer fairt man mit daym owtoh mit daym fahr-rat gayt man tsoo foos
Where are we now?	Wo sind wir jetzt?	Voh zint veer yetst
What is the name of this place?	Wie heisst dieser Ort?	Vee hīst deezer ort
Please show me on the map	Bitte, zeigen Sie mir auf der Karte	Bitter tsīgen zee meer owf dair karter

It's that way	*Da entlang	Dah entlang
It isn't far	*Es ist nicht weit	Es ist nikht vīt
Follow this road for 5 kilometres	*Fahren Sie auf dieser Strasse fünf Kilometer	Fahren zee owf deezer shtrahsser fuinf keeloh-maytair
Keep straight on	*Fahren Sie geradeaus	Fahren zee gayrahder-ows
Turn right at the crossroads	*Biegen Sie bei der Kreuzung nach rechts ab	Beegen zee bī dair kroytsoong nahkh rekhts ap
Take the second road on the left	*Biegen Sie in die zweite Strasse links ein	Beegen zee in dee tsvīter shtrahsser links īn
Turn right at the traffic-lights	*Biegen Sie bei der Verkehrsampel rechts ab	Beegen zee bī dair fer-kayrs-ampel rekhts ap
Turn left after the bridge	*Biegen Sie hinter der Brücke links ab	Beegen zee hintair dair bruiker links ap
The best road is the 35	*Am besten fahren Sie die 35	Am besten fahren zee dee fuinf-oont-drīssig
Go to ... and ask again	*Fahren Sie bis ... und fragen Sie dann wieder	Fahren zee bis ... oont frahgen zee dan veedair
Follow signs for ...	*Folgen Sie dem Schild nach ...	Folgen zee daym shilt nahkh
You are going the wrong way	*Sie gehen falsch	Zee gayen falsh
One-way system	Einbahnverkehr	Īnbahn-fairkayr

North	**Der Norden**	Norden
South	**Der Süden**	Zuiden
East	**Der Osten**	Osten
West	**Der Westen**	Vesten

DRIVING

Have you a road map, please?	Haben Sie bitte eine Strassenkarte?	Hahben zee bitter īner shtrahssenkarter
Where is the nearest car park/garage?	Wo ist der nächste Parkplatz/die nächste Werkstatt?	Voh ist dair naikhster park-plats/dee naikhster verkshtat
(How long) can I park here?	(Wie lange) kann ich hier parken?	(Vee langer) kan ikh heer parken
Have you any change for the meter please?	Haben Sie Kleingeld für den Automaten bitte?	Hahben zee klīngelt fuir dayn owtohmahten bitter
May I see your licence/logbook, please?	*Kann ich bitte Ihren Führerschein/ Kraftfahrzeugschein sehen?	Kan ikh bitter eeren fuir-rer-shīn/kraft-fahr-tsoyg-shīn zayen
Is this your car?	*Ist das Ihr Wagen/ Auto?	Ist das eer vahgen/owtoh

How far is the next petrol station?	Wie weit ist es bis zur nächsten Tankstelle?	Vee vīt ist es bis tsoor naikhsten tank-shtelle
Speed limit	*Geschwindigkeits-grenze	Geshvindikhkīts-grentse
Pedestrian precinct	*Fussgängerzone	Foosgengair-tsohner

CAR HIRE

Where can I hire a car?	Wo kann ich ein Auto mieten?	Voh kan ikh īn owtoh meeten
I want to hire a small/large car	Ich möchte einen kleinen/grossen Wagen mieten	Ikh merkhter īnen klīnen/grohssen vahgen meeten
I want to hire an automatic	Ich möchte einen Automatikwagen mieten	Ikh merkhter īnen owtohmahteekvahgen meeten
I need it for two days/a week	Ich brauche ihn für zwei Tage/eine Woche	Ikh browkher een fuir ts tahger/īner vokher
How much is it by the day/week?	Was kostet es pro Tag/Woche?	Vas kostet es pro tahg/vokher
Is there a weekend rate/a midweek rate?	Haben Sie einen Wochenendtarif/einen Werktagstarif?	Hahben zee īnen vokhen-ent-tahreef/īnen vairktahgstahreef
Does that include mileage?	Ist Kilometergeld im Preis einbegriffen?	Ist keeloh-maytair-gelt ir prīs īn-begriffen
The charge per kilometre is …	*Die Gebühr pro Kilometer ist …	Dee gebuir pro keeloh-maytair ist

Do you want full insurance?	*Möchten Sie eine Vollkasko-versicherung?	Merkhten zee īner foll-kaskoh-fairsikheroong
Do you want a deposit?	Muss ich eine Kaution zahlen?	Moos ikh īner kowtsyohn tsahlen
What is the deposit?	Wieviel muss ich hinterlegen?	Veefeel moos ikh hīntair-laygen
I will pay by credit card	Ich zahle mit Kreditkarte	Ikh tsahler mit kraydeetkarter
May I see your driving licence?	*Kann ich Ihren Führerschein sehen?	Kan ikh eeren fuirair-shīn zayen
Would you sign here, please?	*Unterschreiben Sie hier, bitte	Oontair-shrīben zee heer bitter
Can I return it in ...?	Kann ich ihn in ... zurückbringen?	Kan ikh een in ... tsoo-ruik-bringen
Could you show me the controls/lights, please?	Können Sie mir bitte die Schaltung/Beleuchtung zeigen?	Kernen zee meer bitter dee shaltoong/be-loykhtoong tsīgen

ROAD SIGNS

Anlieger frei	Residents only
Ausfahrt (für Lkws)	Exit (for lorries)
Bahnübergang	Level crossing
Blaue Zone	Restricted parking
Durchgangsverkehr	Through traffic
Einbahnstrasse	One-way street

Einordnen	Get in lane
Fussgänger	Pedestrians only
Gefahr	Danger
Gefährliche Steigung	Steep hill
Gegenverkehr	Two way traffic
Geschwindigkeitsgrenze	Speed limit
Glatteisgefahr	Icy surface
Grenze	Frontier
Halt!	Stop!
Keine Zufahrt	No entry
Kurven	Bends, curves
Langsam (fahren)	(Go) slow
Lawinengefahr	Avalanche area
Licht einschalten	Lights on
Nicht überholen	Overtaking prohibited
Parken nur mit Parkscheiben	Parking discs required
Parken verboten	No parking
Rechts fahren	Keep right
Rollsplitt	Loose chippings
Scheinwerfer einschalten	Headlights on
Schlechte Fahrbahn	Bad surface
Seitenstreifen nicht befahrbar	Soft verges
Steinschlag	Falling rock
Strasse gesperrt	Road blocked
Strassenbau	Roadworks ahead
Strassenglätte	Slippery surface

Überschwemmungsgefahr	Flooding	
Umleitung	Diversion	
Verkehrsampeln	Traffic lights	
Vorfahrt beachten	Give way	
Vorsicht	Caution	
Zoll	Customs	

AT THE GARAGE OR PETROL STATION[1]

Fill it up, please	Voll bitte	Foll bitter
How much is petrol/ diesel a litre?	Wie teuer ist das Benzin/Diesel pro Liter?	Vee toyer ist das bentseen/deezel pro leetair
... litres of standard/ premium petrol, please	... Liter Normal/ Super, bitte	... leetair normahl/super bitter
... marks' worth of petrol, please	Für ... Mark Benzin, bitte	Fuir ... mark bentseen bitter
Please check the oil and water	Bitte prüfen Sie das Öl und das Wasser	Bitter pruifen zee das erl oont das vassair
Could you check the brake/transmission fluid, please?	Prüfen Sie bitte die Bremsflüssigkeit/ Getriebeflüssigkeit	Pruifen zee bitter dee brems-fluissig-kīt/ge-treeber-fluissig-kīt

1. Petrol is more expensive on motorways; you can get a free map of petrol stations just off the motorway that charge lower prices from the ADAC.

Would you clean the windscreen, please?	Machen Sie bitte die Windschutzscheibe sauber	Makhen zee bitter dee vint-shoots-shiber zowbair
The oil needs changing	Das Öl muss gewechselt werden	Das erl moos ge-vekselt vairden
Check the tyre pressures, please	Prüfen Sie bitte den Reifendruck	Pruifen zee bitter dayn rifen-drook
Please wash the car	Bitte waschen Sie den Wagen	Bitter vashen zee dayn vahgen
Can I garage the car here?	Kann ich den Wagen hier einstellen?	Kan ikh dayn vahgen heer inshtellen
What time does the garage close?	Wann wird die Garage geschlossen?	Van veert dee garahjer ge-shlossen
Where are the toilets?	Wo sind die Toiletten?	Voh zint dee twaletten

REPAIRS

My car is broken down	Ich habe eine Autopanne	Ikh hahber iner owtoh-panner
Can you give me a lift to a telephone?	Können Sie mich zu einem Telefon mitnehmen?	Kernen zee mikh tsoo inem telefohn mit-naymen
May I use your phone?	Darf ich Ihr Telefon benutzen?	Darf ikh eer taylefohn benootsen
Where is there a ... agent here?	Wo gibt es eine ... Vertretung?	Voh geept es iner ... fair-traytoong
Have you a breakdown service?	Haben Sie einen Abschleppdienst?	Hahben zee inen apshlep-deenst

Is there a mechanic?	**Haben Sie einen Mechaniker?**	Hahben zee īnen mekhahnikair
Can you send someone to look at it/tow it away?	**Können Sie jemanden schicken, der sich den Wagen ansieht/der den Wagen abschleppt?**	Kernen zee yaymanden shicken dair zikh dayn vahgen anzeet/dair dayn vahgen apshlept
It is an automatic and cannot be towed	**Er hat ein automatisches Getriebe und kann nicht abgeschleppt werden**	Air hat īn owtohmahteeshes getreeber oont kan nikht apgeshlept vairden
Where are you?	***Wo sind Sie?**	Voh zint zee
Where is your car?	***Wo ist Ihr Wagen?**	Voh ist eer vahgen
I'm on the road from ... to ..., near kilometre post ...	**Ich bin auf der Strasse von ... nach ... in der Nähe von Kilometerstein ...**	Ikh bin owf dair shtrahsser fon ... nahkh ... in dair nay-er fon kilomaytershtīn
How long will you be?	**Wie lange wird es dauern?**	Vee langer veert es dow-airn
I want the car serviced	**Ich möchte den Wagen überholen lassen**	Ikh merkhter dayn vahgen uibair-hohlen lassen
The tyre is flat, can you mend it?	**Dieser Reifen ist platt, können Sie ihn reparieren?**	Deezer rīfen ist plat kernen zee een ihn ray-pahreeren
The valve/radiator is leaking	**Das Schlauchventil/ der Kühler ist undicht**	Das shlowkh-venteel/dair kuilair ist oon-dikht

The battery is flat, it needs charging	**Die Batterie ist leer, sie muss aufgeladen werden**	Dee battairee ist layr zee moos **owf**-gelahden vairden
My car won't start	**Mein Wagen fährt nicht an**	Mīne **vah**gen fairt nikht an
It's not running properly	**Er läuft nicht richtig**	Ayr loyft nikht **rikh**tikh
The engine is overheating	**Der Motor läuft sich heiss**	Dair mohtor loyft zikh hīs
Can you change this faulty plug?	**Können Sie diese Zündkerze auswechseln?**	Kernen zee **dee**zer **tsuint**-kertser **ows**-vekseln
There's a petrol/oil leak	**Ich verliere Benzin/Öl**	Ikh fair-**leer**er bent**seen**/erl
There's a smell of petrol/rubber	**Es riecht nach Benzin/Gummi**	Es reekht nahkh bent**seen**/**goo**mee
There's a rattle/squeak	**Es klappert/quietscht**	Es **klap**airt/kveetsht
Something is wrong	**Etwas funktioniert nicht**	Etvas foonktsyon**eert** nikht
with the brakes	**an der Bremse**	an dair **brem**zer
with my car	**an meinem Wagen**	an mīnem **vah**gen
with the clutch	**an der Kupplung**	an dair **koop**loong
with the engine	**an dem Motor**	an daym **moh**tor
with the gearbox	**am Getriebe**	am get**ree**ber
with the lights	**an dem Licht**	an daym likht
with the steering	**an der Steuerung**	an dair **shtoy**-eroong
The exhaust is broken	**Der Auspuff ist kaputt**	Dair **ows**poof ist ka**poot**
The windscreen wipers don't work	**Die Scheibenwischer funktionieren nicht**	Dee **shī**ben-vishair foonktsyon**eeren** nikht

I've got electrical/ mechanical trouble	Der Wagen hat einen elektrischen/ mechanischen Defekt	Dair vahgen hat īnen elektrishen/ mekhahnishen dayfekt
The carburettor needs adjusting	Der Vergaser muss eingestellt werden	Dair fair-gahzer moos īngeshtelt vairden
I've lost my car key	Ich habe meinen Autoschlüssel verloren	Ikh hahber mīnen owtoh-shluissel fair-lohren
Can you repair it?	Können Sie es reparieren?	Kernen zee es ray-pahreeren
How long will it take to repair?	Wie lange wird die Reparatur dauern?	Vee langer veert dee raypah-rahtoor dow-airn
What will it cost?	Wie teuer ist es?	Vee toyair ist es
When can I pick the car up?	Wann kann ich den Wagen abholen?	Van kan ikh dayn vahgen aphohlen
It will take two days	*Es dauert zwei Tage	Es dowairt tsvī tahger
We can repair it temporarily	*Wir können es vorübergehend reparieren	Veer kernen es foh-ruibair-gayhent ray-pahreeren
We haven't the right spares	*Wir haben nicht die richtigen Ersatzteile	Veer hahben nikht dee rikhteegen air-zatstīler
We have to send for the spares	*Wir müssen uns die Ersatzteile schicken lassen	Veer muissen oons dee air-zatstīler shicken lassen
You will need a new ...	*Sie brauchen ein (eine, einen) neues (neue, neuen) ...	Zee browkhen īn (īner, īnen) noyes (noyer, noyen)

| Could I have an itemised bill, please? | Geben Sie mir bitte eine Rechnung mit Einzelangaben | Gayben zee meer bitter iner rekhnoong mit intsel-angahben |

PARTS OF A CAR AND OTHER USEFUL WORDS

accelerate (to)	beschleunigen	beshloynigen
accelerator	das Gaspedal	gaspedahl
anti-freeze	der Frostschutz	frostshoots
automatic transmission	das automatische Getriebe	owtoh-matisher getreeber
axle	die Achse	akser
battery	die Batterie	batteree
bonnet	die Motorhaube	mohtorhowber
boot/trunk	der Gepäckraum	gepeckrowm
brake	die Bremse	bremzer
brake lights	die Bremslichter	bremz-likhtair
brake lining	der Bremsbelag	bremzbelahg
brake pads	die Bremsschuhe	bremz-shooer
breakdown	die Panne	panner
bulb	die Glühbirne	gluibeerner
bumper	die Stoss-stange	shtohss-shtanger
carburettor	der Vergaser	fairgahser
choke	der Choke	tshohk
clutch	die Kupplung	kooploong

cooling system	das Kühlungssystem	kuiloongs-suistaym
cylinder	der Zylinder	tseelinder
differential gear	das Ausgleichgetriebe	owsglïkhgetreeber
dip stick	der Ölmesser	erlmesser
distilled water	das destillierte Wasser	destileerter vasser
distributor	der Verteiler	fairtïler
door	die Tür	tuir
doorhandle	der Türgriff	tuirgrif
drive (to)	fahren	fahren
dynamo	der Dynamo	duinahmoh
engine	der Motor	mohtor
exhaust	der Auspuff	owspoof
fanbelt	der Ventilatorriemen	fenteelahtor-reemen
(oil) filter	der (Öl) Filter	(erl) filter
foglamp	die Nebellampe	naybellamper
fusebox	die Sicherungsdose	zikhairoongsdohzer
gasket	der Dichtungsring	dikhtoongsring
gears	die Gänge	genger
gear-box	das Getriebe	getreeber
gear-lever	der Schalthebel	shalthaybel
grease (to)	schmieren	shmeeren
handbrake	die Handbremse	hantbremzer
headlights	die Scheinwerfer	shïn-vair-fair
heater	die Heizung	hïtsoong
horn	die Hupe	hooper

hose	der Schlauch	shlowkh
ignition	die Zündung	tsuindoong
ignition key	der Zündschlüssel	tsuindshluissel
indicator (flashing)	der Winker	vinker
jack	der Wagenheber	vahgenhayber
lock/catch	das Schloss	shlos
mirror	der Spiegel	shpeegel
number plate	das Nummernschild	noomernshilt
nut	die Mutter	mooter
oil	das Öl	erl
parking lights	das Standlicht/ Parklicht	shtantlikht/parklikht
petrol	das Benzin	bentseen
petrol can	der Benzinkanister	bentseen-kanister
piston	der Kolben	kolben
points	die Kontakte	kontakter
puncture	die Reifenpanne	rīfenpanner
radiator	der Kühler	kuilair
rear lights	das Schlusslicht	shlooslikht
reverse (to)	rückwärts fahren	ruikvairts fahren
reverse gear	der Rückwärtsgang	ruikvairtsgang
reversing lights	die Rückfahrscheinwerfer	ruikfahr-shīn-vairfair
(sliding) roof	das (Schiebe) Dach	(sheeber) dakh
screwdriver	der Schraubenzieher	shrowben-tseeyer
seat	der Sitz	zits
shock absorber	der Stossdämpfer	shtohsdempfer

silencer	der Auspufftopf	owspooftopf
(plug) spanner	der Schrauben-schlüssel	shrowbenshluissel
spares	die Ersatzteile	airsatstïler
speed	die Geschwindigkeit	geshvindikh-kīt
speedometer	der Tachometer	tahkhomayter
spring	die Feder	faydair
stall (to)	stehenbleiben	shtayen-blïben
starter	der Anlasser/Starter	anlasser/shtarter
starter motor	der Anlassermotor	anlassermotor
steering	die Steuerung	shtoyeroong
steering wheel	das Steuerrad	shtoyer-raht
suspension	die Federung	fayderoong
tank	der (Benzin) Tank	(bentseen) tank
tappets	die Stössel	shtersel
transmission	die Kraftübertragung	kraftuiber-trahgoong
tyre	der Reifen	rīfen
valve	das Schlauchventil	shlowkh-fenteel
wheel	das Rad	raht
back	der Hinterreifen	hintair-rīfen
front	der Vorderreifen	fordair-rīfen
spare	der Ersatzreifen	erzats-rīfen
window	das Fenster	fenstair
windscreen	die Windschutzscheibe	vintshoots-shī-ber
windscreen washers	die Scheibenwaschanlage	shïben-vashanlahger
windscreen wipers	der Scheibenwischer	shïben-vishair

CYCLING

Where can I hire a bicycle?	Wo kann ich ein Fahrrad mieten?	Voh kan ikh īn fahrrat meeten
Do you have a bicycle with gears?	Haben Sie ein Fahrrad mit Gangschaltung?	Hahben zee īn fahrraht mit gangshaltoong
The saddle is too high/too low	Der Sattel ist zu hoch/niedrig	Dair zattel ist tsoo hohhk/needrikh
Where is the cycle shop?	Wo ist das Fahrradgeschäft?	Voh ist das fahrrahtgesheft
Do you repair bicycles?	Reparieren Sie Fahrräder?	Raypahreeren zee fahrraydair
The brake isn't working	Die Bremse funktioniert nicht	Dee bremzer foonksyoneert nikht
Could you tighten/loosen the brake cable?	Könnten Sie das Bremskabel anziehen/lockern?	Kernten zee das bremskahbel antsee-en/lokairn
A spoke is broken	Eine Speiche ist kaputt	Īner shpīkher ist kahpoot

The tyre is punctured	Ich habe eine Reifenpanne	Ikh hahber īner rīfenpanner
The gears need adjusting	Die Gänge müssen neu eingestellt werden	Dee genger muissen noy īngeshtellt vairden
Could you straighten the wheel?	Könnten Sie das Rad geraderichten?	Kernten zee das raht gerahder-rikhten
The handlebars are loose	Die Lenkstange ist lose	Dee lenkshtanger ist lohzer
Could you please lend me a spanner/a tyre lever?	Könnten Sie mir bitte einen Schraubenschlüssel/einen Montierhebel leihen?	Kernten zee meer bitter īnen shrowbenshluissel/īnen monteerhaybel līyen?

PARTS OF A BICYCLE

axle	die Achse	akser
bell	die Klingel	klingel
brake (front)	die Vorderbremse	fordair-bremzer
(rear)	die Rückbremse	ruik-bremzer
brake cable	das Bremskabel	bremskahbel
brake lever	der Bremshebel	bremshaybel
bulb	die Birne	birner
chain	die Kette	ketter
dynamo	der Dynamo	duinahmoh
frame	das Gestell	geshtel

gear lever	**der Schalthebel**	shalthaybel
gears	**die Gänge**	genger
handlebars	**die Lenkstange**	lenkshtanger
inner tube	**der Innenreifen**	innenrīfen
light (*front*)	**das Vorderlicht**	fordair-likht
(*rear*)	**das Rücklicht**	ruik-likht
mudguard	**das Schutzblech**	shootsblekh
panniers	**die Packtaschen**	paktashen
pedal	**das Pedal**	paydahl
pump	**die Pumpe**	poomper
reflector	**das Katzenauge**	katsenowger
rim	**der Rand**	rant
saddle	**der Sattel**	zattel
saddlebag	**die Satteltasche**	zattel-tasher
spoke	**die Speiche**	shpīkher
tyre	**der Reifen**	rīfen
valve	**das Ventil**	venteel
wheel	**das Rad**	raht

HOTELS & GUEST HOUSES

BOOKING A ROOM

Rooms to let/vacancies	*Zimmer zu vermieten/Zimmer frei	Tsimmair tsoo fairmeeten/tsimmair frī
No vacancies	*Keine Zimmer frei	Kīner tsimmair frī
Have you a room for the night?	Haben Sie ein Zimmer für die Nacht?	Hahben zee īn tsimmair fuir dee nakht
Do you know another good hotel?	Kennen Sie ein anderes gutes Hotel?	Kennen zee īn andaires gootes hohtel
I've reserved a room; my name is ...	Ich habe ein Zimmer reserviert; mein Name ist ...	Ikh hahber īn tsimmair rayzairveert; mīn nahmer ist

I want a single room with a shower	Ich möchte ein Einzelzimmer mit Dusche	Ikh **merkh**ter īn **īntsel**-tsimmair mit **doosh**er
I want a room with a double bed and a bathroom	Ich möchte ein Doppelzimmer mit Bad	Ikh **merkh**ter īn doppel-tsimmair mit baht
Have you a room with twin beds?	Haben Sie ein Zweibettzimmer?	**Hahb**en zee īn **tsvī**bett-tsimmair
Have you a room with a private toilet?	Haben Sie ein Zimmer mit Privattoilette?	**Hahb**en zee īn tsimmair mit preevaht-twaletter
How long will you be staying?	*Wie lange bleiben Sie?	Vee **lang**er **blī**ben zee
Is it for one night only?	*Ist es nur für eine Nacht?	Ist es noor fuir īner nakht
I want a room	Ich möchte ein Zimmer	Ikh **merkh**ter īn tsimmair
for two or three days	für zwei oder drei Tage	fuir tsvī **ohd**air drī **tah**ger
for a week until Friday	für eine Woche bis Freitag	fuir īner **vokh**er bis **frī**tahg
What floor is the room on?	In welchem Stock ist das Zimmer?	In **velkh**em shtok ist das tsimmair
Is there a lift/elevator?	Gibt es einen Fahrstuhl?	Geept es īnen **fahr**shtool
Are there facilities for the disabled?	Haben Sie Einrichtungen für Behinderte?	**Hahb**en zee īn-rikhtoongen fuir behindairter
Have you a room on the first floor?	Haben Sie ein Zimmer im ersten Stock?	**Hahb**en zee īn tsimmair im **ayr**sten shtok

May I see the room?	**Kann ich bitte das Zimmer sehen?**	Kan ikh **bitter** das tsimmair zayen
I'll take this room	**Ich nehme dieses Zimmer**	Ikh **naymer** deezez tsimmair
I don't like this room	**Dieses Zimmer gefällt mir nicht**	Deezes tsimmair gefellt meer nikht
Have you another one?	**Haben Sie ein anderes?**	Hahben zee īn anderes
I want a quiet room/a bigger room	**Ich möchte ein ruhiges Zimmer/ ein grösseres Zimmer**	Ikh **merkhter** īn **roo-iges** tsimmair/īn grerseres tsimmair
There's too much noise	**Hier ist zu viel Lärm**	Heer ist tsoo feel lerm
I'd like a room with a balcony	**Ich möchte ein Zimmer mit Balkon**	Ikh **merkhter** īn tsimmair mit balkohn
Have you a room looking on to the street?	**Haben Sie ein Zimmer zur Strassenseite?**	Hahben zee īn tsimmair tsoor **shtrahssen-zīter**
Have you a room looking on to the sea?	**Haben Sie ein Zimmer mit Blick auf das Meer?**	Hahben zee īn tsimmair mit blik owf das mayr
Is there a telephone/ radio/television in the room?	**Hat das Zimmer Telefon/Radio/ Fernsehen?**	Hat das tsimmair tele-fohn/rahdeeyoh/ fairnzayen
We've only a double/ twin-bedded room	***Wir haben nur ein Doppelzimmer/ Zweibettzimmer**	Veer hahben noor īn doppel-tsimmair/tsvī-bet-tsimmair

This is the only room vacant	*Dies ist das einzige freie Zimmer	Dees ist das īntsiger frīyer tsimmair
We shall have another room tomorrow	*Morgen wird ein anderes Zimmer frei	Morgen veert īn anderes tsimmair frī
The room is only available tonight	*Das Zimmer ist nur für heute Nacht frei	Das tsimmair ist noor fuir hoyter nakht frī
How much is the room per night?	Wieviel kostet das Zimmer pro Nacht?	Veefeel kostet das tsimmair pro nakht
Have you nothing cheaper?	Haben Sie nichts Billigeres?	Hahben zee nikhts billigeres
It's too expensive	Es ist zu teuer	Es ist tsoo toyer
What do we pay for the child(ren)?	Was müssen wir für das Kind (die Kinder) bezahlen?	Vas muissen veer fuir das kint (dee kindair) betsahlen
Could you put a cot in the room?	Könnten Sie ein Kinderbett ins Zimmer stellen?	Kernten zee īn kindair-bet ins tsimmair shtellen
Is the service (and tax[1]) included?	Ist Bedienung (und Kurtaxe) einbegriffen?	Ist bedeenoong (oont koortakser) īnbegriffen
Are meals included?	Sind die Mahlzeiten einbegriffen?	Sint dee mahltsīten īnbegriffen
How much is the room without meals?	Wieviel kostet das Zimmer ohne Mahlzeiten?	Veefeel kostet das tsimmair ohner mahltsīten

1. In health resorts only.

How much is the room with full board/with bed and breakfast only?	Wieviel kostet das Zimmer mit Vollpension/nur mit Frühstück?	Veefeel kostet das tsimmair mit foll-pangzeeyohn/noor mit frui-shstuik
Do you do bed and breakfast?	Haben Sie Zimmer mit Frühstück?	Hahben zee tsimmair mit frui-shtuik
Do you have a weekly rate?	Haben Sie einen festen Preis pro Woche?	Hahben zee īnen festen prīs pro vokher
What is the weekly rate?	Was kostet es pro Woche?	Vas kostet es pro vokher
Would you fill in the registration form, please?	*Füllen Sie bitte dieses Anmeldeformular aus	Fuillen zee bitter deezes anmelder-formoolahr ows
Could I have your passport, please?	*Könnte ich bitte Ihren Pass haben?	Kernter ikh bitter eeren pas hahben

IN YOUR ROOM

Chambermaid	Das Zimmermädchen	Tsimmair-maytkhen
Room service	Die Zimmerbedienung	Dee tsimmair-bedeenoong
I'd like breakfast in my room, please	Ich möchte bitte Frühstück in meinem Zimmer haben	Ikh merkhter bitter frui-shtuick in mīnem tsimmair hahben
I'd like some ice cubes	Ich möchte ein paar Eiswürfel	Ikh merkhter īn pahr īs-vuirfel

There's no ashtray in my room	In meinem Zimmer ist kein Aschenbecher	In mīnem tsimmair ist kīn ashen-bekher
Can I have more hangers, please?	Kann ich bitte mehr Kleiderbügel haben?	Kan ikh bitter mayr klīder-buigel hahben
Is there a point for an electric razor?	Gibt es eine Steckdose für Rasierapparate?	Geept es īner shtek-dohzer fuir razeer-aparahter
What's the voltage?	Wie hoch ist die Spannung?	Vee hohkh ist dee shpanoong
Where is the bathroom?	Wo ist das Badezimmer?	Voh ist das bahder-tsimmair
Where is the lavatory?	Wo ist die Toilette?	Voh ist dee twaletter
Is there a shower?	Gibt es eine Dusche?	Geept es īner doosher
There are no towels in my room	In meinem Zimmer sind keine Handtücher	In mīnem tsimmair zint kīner hant-tuikher
There's no soap	Es gibt keine Seife	Es geept kīner sīfer
There's no (hot) water	Es gibt kein (heisses) Wasser	Es geept kīn (hīsses) vassair
There's no plug in my washbasin	In meinem Waschbecken ist kein Stöpsel	In mīnem vashbecken ist kīn shterpsel
There's no toilet paper in the lavatory	In der Toilette ist kein Papier	In dair twaletter ist kīn papeer
The lavatory won't flush	Die Spülung in der Toilette funktioniert nicht	Dee shpuiloong in dair twaletter foonk-tsyoneert nikht
The bidet leaks	Das Bidet ist undicht	Das beeday ist oondikht

May I have the key to the bathroom, please?	Kann ich bitte den Schlüssel fürs Badezimmer haben?	Kan ikh bitter dayn shluissel fuirs bahder-tsimmair hahben
The light doesn't work	Das Licht funktioniert nicht	Das likht foonktsyoneert nikht
The lamp is broken	Die Lampe ist kaputt	Dee lamper ist kahpoot
The blind is stuck	Die Jalousie hat sich verklemmt	Dee jaloozee hat zikh fairklemt
The curtains won't close	Die Vorhänge schliessen nicht	Dee fohrhenger shleessen nikht
May I have another blanket and sheet?	Kann ich bitte noch eine Wolldecke und ein Bettlaken haben?	Kan ikh bitter nokh īner voll-decker oont īn betlahken hahben
May I have another pillow?	Kann ich bitte noch ein Kopfkissen haben?	Kan ikh bitter nokh īn kopf-kissen hahben
I can't sleep under a continental quilt	Ich kann nicht unter einem Federbett schlafen	Ikh kan nikht oonter īnem fayderbet shlahfen
This sheet is dirty	Dieses Bettlaken ist schmutzig	Deezes betlahken ist shmootsikh
I can't open my window; please open it	Ich kann mein Fenster nicht aufmachen; bitte öffnen Sie es für mich	Ikh kan mīn fenstair nikht owf-makhen bitter erfnen zee es fuir mikh
It's too hot/cold	Es ist zu heiss/kalt	Es ist tsoo hīs/kalt

Can the heating be turned up?	Kann die Heizung weiter aufgedreht werden?	Kan dee hītsoong vītair owfgedrayt vairden
Can the heating be turned down?	Kann die Heizung etwas mehr abgedreht werden?	Kan dee hītsoong etvas mayr apgedrayt vairden
Is the room air-conditioned?	Hat das Zimmer Klima-anlage?	Hat das tsimmair kleemah-anlahger
The air conditioning doesn't work	Die Klima-anlage funktioniert nicht	Dee kleemah-anlahger foonktsyoneert nikht
Come in	Herein	Hairīn
Put it on the table, please	Stellen Sie es bitte auf den Tisch	Shtellen zee es bitter owf dayn tish
How long will the laundry take?	Wann ist die Wäsche fertig?	Van ist dee vesher fairtikh
Have you a needle and thread?	Haben Sie Nadel und Faden?	Hahben zee nahdel oont fahden
I want these shoes cleaned	Lassen Sie bitte diese Schuhe putzen	Lassen zee bitter deezer shooer pootsen
I want this dress cleaned	Lassen Sie bitte dieses Kleid reinigen	Lassen zee bitter deezes klīt rīneegen
I want this suit pressed	Lassen Sie bitte diesen Anzug bügeln	Lassen zee bitter deezen antsoog buigeln
When will it be ready?	Wann wird er fertig sein?	Van veert ayr fairtikh zīn
It will be ready tomorrow	*Es wird morgen fertig sein	Es veert morgen fairtikh zīn

OTHER SERVICES

Porter	**Der Portier**	Portyay
Page	**Der Page**	Pahjer
Manager	**Der Manager**	Menejair
Telephonist	**Die Telephonistin**	Taylayfohnistin
My key, please	**Meinen Schlüssel bitte**	Mīnen shluissel bitter
Have you a map of the town/an amusement guide?	**Haben Sie einen Stadtplan/ein Veranstaltungsprogramm?**	Hahben zee īnen shtatplahn/in fairanshtaltoongsprogram
Can I leave this in your safe?	**Könnten Sie dies in Ihren Tresor (Safe) legen?**	Kernten zee dees in eeren trayzohr (sayf) laygen
Are there any letters for me?	**Sind Briefe für mich da?**	Zint breefer fuir mikh dah
Please post this	**Bitte geben Sie dies zur Post**	Bitter gayben zee dees tsoor post
Is there a telex?	**Haben Sie Telexanschluss?**	Hahben zee taylexanshloos
Is there any message for me?	**Ist eine Nachricht für mich da?**	Ist īner nakhrikht fuir mikh dah
If anyone phones, tell them I'll be back at 5.30	**Wenn jemand anruft, sagen Sie bitte, ich bin um halb sechs wieder zurück**	Ven yaymant anrooft zahgen zee bitter ikh bin oom halp zeks veedair tsooruik
No one telephoned	***Es hat niemand angerufen**	Es hat neemant angeroofen

There's a lady/ gentleman to see you	*Eine Dame/ein Herr möchte Sie sprechen	Īner dahmer/īn hair merkhter zee shprekhen
Please ask her/him to come up	Bitten Sie sie/ihn heraufzukommen	Bitten zee zee/een hairowf-tsoo-kommen
I'm coming down (at once)	Ich komme hinunter	Ikh kommer hinoontair
Have you any writing paper? envelopes? stamps?	Haben Sie Papier? Umschläge? Briefmarken?	Hahben zee papeer? oomshlaiger? breefmarken?
Please send the chambermaid/the waiter	Schicken Sie mir bitte das Zimmermädchen/ den Kellner	Shiken zee meer bitter das tsimmair-maytkhen/dayn kellnair
I need a guide/an interpreter	Ich brauche einen Fremdenführer/ einen Dolmetscher	Ikh browkher īnen fremdenfuirer/īnen dolmetshair
Can I borrow a typewriter?	Können Sie mir eine Schreibmaschine leihen?	Kernen zee meer īner shrīb-mash-eener līyen
Does the hotel have a baby-sitting service?	Haben Sie einen Babysitter im Haus	Hahben zee īnen baybeesitter im hows
Where is the dining room?	Wo ist der Speisesaal?	Voh ist dair shpīzer-zahl?
What time is breakfast/lunch/ dinner?	Wann wird das Frühstück/das Mittagessen/das Abendessen serviert?	Van veert das frui-shtuik/das mittahgessen/das ahbentessen sairveert

Where are the toilets/ the cloakroom?	Wo ist die Toilette/ die Garderobe?	Voh ist dee twaletter/dee garderohber
Is there a garage?	Gibt es eine Garage?	Geept es īner garahjer
Where can I park the car?	Wo kann ich den Wagen parken?	Voh kan ikh dayn vahgen parken
Is the hotel open all night?	Ist das Hotel die ganze Nacht offen?	Ist das hohtel dee gantser nakht offen
What time does it close?	Wann wird es abgeschlossen?	Van veert es apgeshlossen
Please wake me at ...	Bitte wecken Sie mich um ...	Bitter vecken zee mikh oom

DEPARTURE

I want to leave tomorrow	Ich möchte morgen abfahren	Ikh merkhter morgen apfahren
Can you have my bill ready?	Können Sie bitte meine Rechnung fertig machen?	Kernen zee bitter mīner rekhnoong fairtikh makhen
Do you accept credit cards?	Nehmen Sie Kreditkarten?	Naymen zee kraydeet-karten
There is a mistake on the bill	Die Rechnung stimmt nicht	Dee rekhnoong shtimt nikht
I shall be coming back on ..., can I book a room for that date?	Ich komme am ... zurück, kann ich für die Zeit ein Zimmer reservieren?	Ikh kommer am ... tsooruick kan ikh fuir dee tsīt īn tsimmair raizairveeren

Please store the luggage, we will be back at ...	Bitte bewahren Sie das Gepäck auf, wir kommen um ... zurück	Bitter bevahren zee das gepeck owf veer kommen oom ... tsooruik
Could you have my luggage brought down?	Können Sie bitte mein Gepäck runterbringen lassen?	Kernen zee bitter min gepeck roontair-bringen lassen
Please order a taxi for me	Bitte bestellen Sie mir ein Taxi	Bitter beshtellen zee meer in tacksee
Thank you for a pleasant stay	Vielen Dank für den angenehmen Aufenthalt	Feelen dank fuir dayn angenaymen owfent-halt

CAMPING

Is there a camp site nearby?	Ist hier in der Nähe ein Campingplatz?	Ist heer in dair **nayer** īn kampingplats
May we camp here in your field/on the beach?	Können wir hier auf Ihrem Feld/am Strand zelten?	Kernen veer heer owf eerem felt/am shtrant tselten
Where should we put our tent/caravan?	Wo sollen wir mit unserem Zelt/ Wohnwagen hin?	Voh zollen veer mit oonzerem tselt/ vohnvahgen hin
Can I park the car next to the tent?	Kann ich den Wagen neben dem Zelt parken?	Kan ikh dayn **vahgen** nayben daym tselt parken
Can we hire a tent?	Können wir ein Zelt mieten?	Kernen veer īn tselt meeten
Is there drinking water? electricity? showers? toilets?	Gibt es hier Trinkwasser? Elektrizität? Duschen? Toiletten?	Geept es heer trinkvassair aylektreetseetayt dooshen twaletten

What does it cost
  per night?
  per week?
  per person?
	Wieviel kostet es
	  pro Nacht?
	  pro Woche?
	  pro Person?
		Veefeel kostet es
		  pro Nacht?
		  pro vokher
		  pro pairzohn

On the site, is there	Gibt es auf dem Platz	Geept es owf daym plats

a shop?
  a swimming pool?
  a playground?
  a restaurant?
  a launderette?
	ein Geschäft?
	  ein Schwimmbad?
	  einen Spielplatz?
	  ein Restaurant?
	  eine
	  Münzwäscherei?
		īn gesheft
		  īn shvimbaht
		  īnen shpeelplats
		  īn restohrang
		  īner muintsveshairī

Can I buy ice?	Kann ich Eis kaufen	Kan ikh īs kowfen

Where can I buy
  paraffin/butane gas?
	Wo kann ich
	  Petroleum/Butan
	  (Gas) kaufen?
		Voh kan ikh
		  paytrohlayoom/
		  bootahn (gas) kowfen

Where do I put
  rubbish?
	Wo kommt der
	  Abfall hin?
		Voh kommt dair apfall hin

Where can I wash up/
  wash clothes?
	Wo kann ich
	  abwaschen/mein
	  Zeug waschen?
		Voh kan ikh apvashen/
		  mīn tsoyg vashen

Is there somewhere to
  dry clothes/
  equipment?
	Wo kann ich mein
	  Zeug/meine
	  Ausrüstung
	  trocknen?
		Voh kan ikh mīn tsoyg/
		  mīner owsruistoong
		  troknen

My camping gas has
  run out
	Ich habe kein
	  Campinggas mehr
		Ikh hahber kīn
		  kamping-gas mayr

The toilet is blocked	Die Toilette ist
	  verstopft
		Dee twaletter ist
		  fairshtopft

The shower doesn't work/is flooded	**Die Dusche funktioniert nicht/ist überschwemmt**	Dee **doosh**her **foonkt**syoneert nikht/ist uibairshvemmt
What is the voltage?	**Wie ist die (Strom) Spannung hier?**	Vee ist dee (shtrohm) **shpan**noong heer
May we light a fire?	**Können wir ein Feuer anmachen?**	**Ker**nen veer in **foyair** **an**makhen
Please prepare the bill, we are leaving today	**Bitte stellen Sie die Rechnung aus, wir fahren heute ab**	**Bit**ter **shtel**len zee dee **rekh**noong ows veer **fah**ren **hoy**ter ap
How long do you want to stay?	***Wie lange wollen Sie bleiben?***	Vee **lang**er **vol**len zee **blī**ben
What is your car registration number?	***Wie ist Ihre Autonummer?***	Vee ist **eer**er **ow**tohnoommair
I'm afraid the camp site is full	***Der Campingplatz ist leider voll***	Dair **kamp**ingplats ist **lī**dair foll
No camping	***Camping verboten***	**Kamp**ing fair**boh**ten

YOUTH HOSTELLING

How long is the walk to the youth hostel?	Wie lange geht man zur Jugendherberge?	Vee langer gayt man tsoor yoogenthairbairger
Is there a youth hostel here?	Gibt es hier eine Jugendherberge?	Geept es heer īner yoogenthairbairger
Have you a room/bed for the night?	Haben Sie ein Zimmer/Bett für die Nacht?	Hahben zee īn tsimmair/bet fuir dee nakht
How many days can we stay?	Wieviele Tage können wir bleiben?	Veefeeler tahger kernen veer blīben
Here is my membership card	Hier ist meine Mitgliedskarte	Heer ist mīner mitgleedskarter
Do you serve meals?	Servieren Sie Essen?	Zairveeren zee essen
Can I use the kitchen?	Kann ich die Küche benutzen?	Kan ikh dee kuikher benootsen

| Is there somewhere cheap to eat nearby? | Kann man hier in der Nähe billig essen? | Kan man heer in dair nayer billikh essen |
| I want to rent a sheet for my sleeping bag | Ich möchte ein Laken für meinen Schlafsack mieten | Ikh merkhter īn lahken fuir mīnen shlahfzak meeten |

RENTING A PLACE

We have rented an apartment/villa	**Wir haben eine Wohnung/Villa gemietet**	Veer hahben īner vohnoong/villah gemeetet
Here is our reservation	**Hier ist unsere Reservierung**	Heer ist oonzerer rayzairveeroong
Please show us around	**Bitte zeigen Sie uns die Wohnung/Villa**	Bitter tsīgen zee oons dee vohnoong/villah
Is the cost of electricity/the gas cylinder/the maid included?	**Ist der Strom/der Gaszylinder/das (Dienst) Mädchen mit (im Preis) einbegriffen?**	Ist dair shtrohm/dair gas-tsilindair/das deenst-maytkhen mit (im prīs) īnbegriffen

YOUTH HOSTELLING · 73

Where is the electricity mains switch?	Wo ist der Schalter für die Hauptstrom-leitung?	Voh ist dair shaltair fuir dee howptshtrom-lītoong
water mains stopcock?	der Hauptwasser-leitungshahn?	dair howptvassair-lītoongshahn
light switch?	der Lichtschalter?	dair likhtshaltair
powerpoint?	der Steck-kontakt?	dair shtek-kontakt
fuse box?	der Sicherungs-kasten?	dair zikhairoongs-kasten
How does the heating/hot water work?	Wie funktioniert die Heizung/das warme Wasser?	Vee foonktsyoneert dee hītsoong/das varmer vassair
Is there a spare gas cylinder?	Ist da noch ein Ersatzgaszylinder?	Ist dah nokh īn airzats-gas-tsilindair
Do gas cylinders get delivered?	Werden Gaszylinder ins Haus geliefert?	Vairden gas-tsilindair ins hows geleefairt
Please show me how this works	Bitte zeigen Sie mir, wie dies funktioniert	Bitter tsīgen zee meer vee dees foonktsyoneert
Which days does the maid come?	An welchen Tagen kommt das Dienstmädchen?	An velkhen tahgen kommt das deenstmaytkhen
For how long?	Für wie lange?	Fuir vee langer
Is there a fly-screen?	Gibt es ein Fliegenfenster?	Geept es īn fleegenfenstair
When is the rubbish collected?	Wann wird der Abfall abgeholt?	Van veert dair apfall apgehohlt
Where can we buy logs for the fire?	Wo können wir Feuerholz kaufen?	Voh kernen veer foyair holts kowfen

Is there a barbecue?	Gibt es ein Barbecue?	Geept es īn barbekyoo
Please give me another set of keys	Bitte geben Sie mir noch Ersatzschlüssel	Bitter gayben zee meer nokh airzatsshluissel
We have replaced the broken china	Wir haben das zerbrochene Geschirr ersetzt	Veer hahben das tsairbrokhener geshirr airzetst
Here is the bill	Hier ist die Rechnung	Heer ist dee rekhnoong
Please return my deposit against breakages	Bitte zahlen Sie mir meine Kaution zurück	Bitter tsahlen zee meer mīner kowtsyohn tsooruick

PROBLEMS

The drain/the pipe/the sink is blocked	Der Abfluss/das Rohr/der Ausguss ist verstopft	Dair apfloos/das rohr/dair owsgoos ist fairshtopft
The toilet doesn't flush	Die Toilettenspülung funktioniert nicht	Dee twaletten-shpuiloong foonktsyoneert nikht
There's no water	Wir haben kein Wasser	Veer hahben kīn vassair
We can't turn the water off/the shower on	Wir können das Wasser nicht abdrehen/die Dusche nicht andrehen	Veer kernen das vassair nikht apdrehen/dee doosher nikht andrehen
There is a leak	Etwas ist undicht	Etvas ist oondikht

There is a broken window	Eine Fensterscheibe ist zerbrochen	Iner fenstairshiber ist tsairbrokhen
The shutters won't close	Die Fensterläden schliessen nicht	Dee fenstairlayden shleessen nikht
The window won't open	Das Fenster geht nicht auf	Das fenstair gayt nikht owf
The electricity has gone off	Der Strom ist abgeschaltet	Dair shtrohm ist apgeshaltet
The heating	Die Heizung	Dee hi-tsoong
The cooker	Der Herd	Dair hayrt
The refrigerator	Der Kühlschrank	Dair kuihlshrank
The water heater	Der Durchlauf-erhitzer	Dair doorkhlowf-airhitsair
... doesn't work	... funktioniert nicht	... foonktsyoneert nikht
The lock is stuck	Das Schloss klemmt	Das shloss klemt
This is broken	Dies ist kaputt	Dees ist kahpoot
This needs repairing	Dies muss repariert werden	Dees moos raypahreert vairden
The apartment/villa has been burgled	In die Wohnung/Villa ist eingebrochen worden	In dee vohnoong/villah ist ingebrokhen vorden

MEETING PEOPLE

How are you/things?	**Wie geht es Ihnen?/ Wie steht's?**	Vee gayt es eenen/vee shtayts
Fine, thanks, and you?	**Gut, danke, und Ihnen?**	Goot danker oont eenen
May I introduce ...?	**Darf ich ... vorstellen?**	Darf ikh ... fohrshtellen
My name is ...	**Mein Name ist ...**	Mīn nahmer ist
Have you met ...?	**Kennen Sie ...?**	Kennen zee
Glad to meet you	**Es freut mich, Sie kennenzulernen/** (*more emphatic*) **Angenehm**	Es froyt mikh zee kennentsoo-lairnen/ angenaym
Am I disturbing you?	**Störe ich Sie?**	Shterer ikh zee
Go away	**Gehen Sie weg**	Gayen zee vekh
Leave me alone	**Lassen Sie mich in Ruhe**	Lassen zee mikh in roo-er
Sorry to have troubled you	**Entschuldigen Sie die Störung**	Entshooldigen zee dee shteroong

MAKING FRIENDS

Do you travel a lot?	**Reisen Sie viel?**	Rīzen zee feel
We've been here a week	**Wir sind seit einer Woche hier**	Veer zint zīt īnair vokher heer
Do you live/are you staying here?	**Wohnen Sie hier?**	Vohnen zee heer
Is this your first visit here?	**Sind Sie zum erstenmal hier?**	Zint zee tsoom airstenmahl heer
Do you like it here?	**Gefällt es Ihnen hier?**	Gefellt es eenen heer
Are you on your own?	**Sind Sie allein(e)?**	Zint zee allīn(er)
I am with my husband	**Ich bin mit meinem Mann**	Ikh bin mit mīnem man
my wife	**meiner Frau hier**	mīnair frow heer
my parents	**meinen Eltern**	mīnen eltairn
my family	**meiner Familie**	mīnair fameeleeyer
a friend	**einem Freund/ einer Freundin**	īnem froynt/īnair froyndin
I am travelling alone	**Ich reise allein**	Ikh rīzer allīn
Are you married/ single?	**Sind Sie verheiratet/ledig?**	Zint zee fairhīrahtet/ laydikh
Do you have children?	**Haben Sie Kinder?**	Hahben zee kindair
Where do you come from?	**Woher sind Sie?**	Vo-**hair** zint zee
I come from ...	**Ich komme aus ...**	Ikh kommer ows
What do you do?	**Was machen Sie beruflich?**	Vas **makh**en zee be**roof**likh

What are you studying?	Was studieren Sie?	Vas shtoodeeren zee
I'm on holiday/a (business) trip	Ich bin auf Urlaub/geschäftlich hier	Ikh bin owf oorlowp/gesheftlikh heer
Have you been to England/America?	Sind Sie schon in England/Amerika gewesen?	Zint zee shohn in englant/amayreekah gevayzen
I hope to see you again	Ich hoffe, wir sehen uns wieder	Ikh hoffer veer zayen oons veedair
Do you smoke?	Rauchen Sie?	Rowkhen zee
No, I don't, thanks	Nein, ich rauche nicht, danke	Nīn ikh rowkher nikht danker
I have given it up	Ich habe es aufgegeben	Ikh hahber es owfgegayben
Help yourself	Bedienen Sie sich	Bedeenen zee zikh
Can I get you a drink?	Kann ich Ihnen etwas zu trinken holen?	Kan ikh eenen etvas tsoo trinken hohlen
I'd like a ... please	Ich hätte gern ...	Ikh hetter gairn

INVITATIONS

Would you like to have lunch tomorrow?	Sollen wir morgen zusammen Mittag essen?	Zollen veer morgen tsoozammen mittahg essen
I'd love to come	Ich komme gern	Ikh kommer gairn
I'm sorry, I can't come	Leider kann ich nicht kommen	Līdair kan ikh nikht kommen

Are you doing anything tonight/tomorrow afternoon?	Haben Sie heute Abend/morgen Nachmittag etwas vor?	Hahben zee hoyter ahbent/morgen nakhmittakh etvas fohr
Could we have coffee/a drink somewhere?	Können wir irgendwo einen Kaffee trinken/ etwas trinken?	Kernen veer eergentvoh īnen kaffay trinken/ etvas trinken
Shall we go to the cinema/theatre?	Sollen wir ins Kino/ Theater gehen?	Zollen veer ins keenoh/ tay-ahtair gayen
Shall we go to the beach?	Wollen wir an den Strand fahren?	Vollen veer an dayn shtrant fahren
Would you like to go dancing/for a drive?	Möchten Sie tanzen gehen/ausfahren?	Merkhten zee tantsen gayen/owsfahren
Do you know a good disco/restaurant?	Kennen Sie eine gute Diskothek/ein gutes Restaurant?	Kennen zee īner gooter diskoh-tayk/īn gootes restorant
Can you come to dinner/for a drink?	Können Sie zum Abendessen/auf ein Gläschen zu uns kommen?	Kernen zee tsoom ahbentessen/owf īn gleskhen tsoo oons kommen
We're giving/there is a party. Would you like to come?	Wir geben/es gibt eine Party. Möchten Sie auch kommen?	Veer gayben/es geept īner partee merkhten zee owkh kommen
May I bring a (girl) friend?	Kann ich einen Freund (eine Freundin) mitbringen?	Kan ikh īnen froynt (īner froyndin) mitbringen
Thanks for the invitation	Vielen Dank für die Einladung	Feelen dank fuir dee īnlahdoong

Where shall we meet?	Wo sollen wir uns treffen?	Voh zollen veer oons treffen
What time shall I/we come?	Wann soll ich/sollen wir kommen?	Van zoll ikh/zollen veer kommen
I could pick you up at ... (time/place)	Ich könnte Sie um ... von ... abholen	Ikh kernter zee oom ... fon ... aphohlen
Could we meet at ...?	Könnten wir uns um ... treffen?	Kernten veer oons oom ... treffen
May I see you home?	Darf ich Sie nach Hause begleiten?	Darf ikh zee nahkh howzer beglīten
Can we give you a lift home/to your hotel?	Können wir Sie nach Hause/zu Ihrem Hotel fahren?	Kernen veer zee nahkh howzer/tsoo eerem hohtel fahren
Can I see you again?	Können wir uns wiedersehen?	Kernen veer oons veederzayen
Where do you live?	Wo wohnen Sie?	Voh vohnen zee
What is your telephone number?	Wie ist Ihre Telefonnummer?	Vee ist eerer taylefohn-noomair
Thanks for the evening/nice time	Vielen Dank für den netten Abend/die netten Stunden	Feelen dank fuir dayn netten ahbent/dee netten shtoonden
It was lovely	Es war sehr nett	Es vahr zayr nett
Hope to see you again soon	Hoffentlich sehen wir uns bald wieder	Hoffentlikh zayen veer oons balt veedair
See you soon/later/tomorrow	Bis bald/später/morgen	Bis balt/shpaytair/morgen

GOING TO A RESTAURANT

Can you suggest	Können Sie	Kernen zee
a good restaurant	ein gutes Restaurant	īn gootes restorant
a cheap restaurant	ein billiges Restaurant	īn billiges restorant
a vegetarian restaurant?	ein vegetarisches Restaurant vorschlagen?	īn faygetahrishes restorant fohrshlahgen
I'd like to book a table for four at 1 p.m.	Ich möchte einen Tisch für vier Personen für ein Uhr bestellen	Ikh merkhter īnen tish fuir feer pairzohnen fuir īn oor beshtellen
I've reserved a table; my name is …	Ich habe einen Tisch reserviert; mein Name ist …	Ikh hahber īnen tish rayzerveert; mīn nahmer ist
We did not make a reservation	Wir haben keinen Tisch reserviert	Veer hahben kīnen tish rayzerveert

Is there a table on the terrace/by the window/in a corner?	**Haben Sie einen Tisch auf der Terrasse/beim Fenster/in der Ecke?**	Hahben zee īnen tish owf dair tairrasser/bīm fenstair/in dair ecker
Is there a non-smoking area?	**Gibt es einen Nichtraucher-bereich?**	Geept es īnen nikht-rowkher bairīkh
This way, please	***Hier entlang bitte**	Heer entlang bitter
We shall have a table free in half an hour	***In einer halben Stunde haben wir einen Tisch frei**	In īnair halben shtoonder haben veer īnen tish frī
We don't serve lunch until 12.30	***Das Mittagessen wird erst um halb eins serviert**	Das mittahg-essen veert airst oom halp īnts zairveert
We don't serve dinner until 8 p.m.	***Das Abendessen wird erst um acht Uhr serviert**	Das ahbent-essen veert airst oom akht oor zairveert
We stop serving at 9 o'clock	***Wir servieren nur bis neun Uhr**	Veer zairveeren noor bis noyn oor
Sorry, the kitchen is closed	***Es tut mir leid, die Küche ist geschlossen**	Es toot meer līt dee kuīkher ist geshlossen
Where is the cloakroom?	**Wo ist die Toilette?**	Voh ist dee twaletter
It is downstairs	***Die Toiletten sind unten**	Dee twaletten zint oonten

ORDERING

Service charge	*Bedienungsgeld	Bedeenoongs-gelt
Service and V.A.T. not included	*Bedienung und Mehrwehrtsteuer nicht einbegriffen	Bedeenoong oont mayr-vairt-shtoyair nikht īnbegriffen
Service and V.A.T. included	*(Unsere Preise sind) Endpreise	(Oonzerer prīzer zint) entprīzer
Cover charge	*Gedeck	Gedeck
Waiter/waitress (address)	Ober/Fräulein	Ohbair/froylīn
May I see the menu/ the wine list, please?	Darf ich bitte die Speisekarte/die Weinkarte sehen?	Darf ikh bitter dee shpīzer-karter/dee vīn-karter zayen
Is there a set menu?	Gibt es ein Tagesgedeck?	Geept es īn tahges-gedeck
I want something light	Ich möchte eine leichte Kost	Ikh merkhter īner līkhter kost
We are in a hurry	Wir haben es eilig	Veer hahben es īlikh
Do you serve snacks?	Servieren Sie einen Imbiss?	Zairveeren zee īnen imbiss
Do you have children's helpings?	Haben Sie Kinderportionen?	Hahben zee kindair-portseeohnen
What is your dish of the day?	Was ist Ihre Tagesspezialität?	Vas ist eerer tahges-shpaytseeyalitayt
What do you recommend?	Was empfehlen Sie?	Vas empfaylen zee
Can you tell me what this is?	Können Sie mir sagen, was dies ist?	Kernen zee meer zahgen vas dees ist

What is the speciality of the restaurant/of the region?	Was ist die Spezialität dieses Restaurants/dieser Gegend?	Vas ist dee shpaytseeyalitayt deezes restorants/ deezair gaygent
Do you have any local dishes/vegetarian dishes?	Haben Sie hiesige Gerichte/ vegetarische Gerichte?	Hahben zee hee-zee-ger ge-rikh-ter/ vegetahreesher ge-rikh-ter
Would you like to try ...?	*Möchten Sie ... probieren?	Merkhten zee ... prohbeeren
There's no more ...	*... sind (ist) nicht mehr da	... zint (ist) nikht mayr dah
I'd like ...	Ich möchte ...	Ikh merkhter
May I have peas instead of beans?	Darf ich Erbsen statt Bohnen haben?	Darf ikh airpsen shtat bohnen hahben
Without oil/sauce, please	Ohne Sauce/Öl bitte	Ohner sohser/erl bitter
Some more bread, please	Noch etwas Brot bitte	Nokh etvas broht bitter
A little more ...	Etwas mehr ...	Etvas mayr
Is it hot or cold?	Ist es warm oder kalt?	Ist es varm ohdair kalt
Where are our drinks?	Wo sind unsere Getränke?	Voh zint oonzerer getrenker

COMPLAINTS

| Why is the food taking so long? | Warum müssen wir so lange auf unser Essen warten? | Vahroom muissen veer zoh langer owf oonzair essen varten |

This isn't what I ordered, I want ...	Das habe ich nicht bestellt, ich möchte ...	Das hahber ikh nikht beshtellt ikh merkhter
This is bad	Dies ist schlecht	Dees ist shlekht
This isn't fresh	Dies ist nicht frisch	Dees ist nikht frish
This is uncooked/overcooked	Dies ist nicht gar/zu lange gekocht	Dees ist nikht gahr/tsoo langer gekokht
This is stale	Dies ist alt/schal	Dees ist alt/shahl
This is too cold/salty	Dies ist zu kalt/salzig	Dees ist tsoo kalt/saltsikh
This plate/knife/spoon/glass is not clean	Dieser Teller/dieses Messer/dieser Löffel/dieses Glas ist nicht sauber	Deezair tellair/deezes messair/deezair lerffel/deezes glas ist nikht zowbair
I'd like to see the headwaiter	Ich möchte den Oberkellner sprechen	Ikh merkhte dayn ohberkellner shprekhen

PAYING

The bill, please	Die Rechnung bitte/Ich möchte zahlen	Dee rekhnoong bitter/ikh merkhter tsahlen
Does it include service?	Ist Bedienung einbegriffen?	Ist bedeenoong inbegriffen
Please check the bill; I don't think it's correct	Bitte prüfen Sie die Rechnung; ich glaube, sie stimmt nicht	Bitter pruifen zee dee rekhnoong ikh glowber zee shtimmt nikht
What is this amount for?	Wofür ist dieser Betrag?	Vohfuir ist deezair betrahg

I didn't have soup	Ich habe keine Suppe gehabt	Ikh hahber kīner zoopper gehapt
I had chicken not beef	Ich hatte Huhn, nicht Rindfleisch	Ikh hatter hoon nikht rint-flīsh
May we have separate bills?	Können wir bitte getrennte Rechnungen haben?	Kernen veer bitter getrennter rekhnoongen hahben
Do you take credit cards/travellers' cheques?	Nehmen Sie Kreditkarten/ Reiseschecks?	Naymen zee kraydeet-karten/rīzer-shecks
Keep the change	Das ist gut so	Das ist goot zoh
It was very good	Es war sehr gut	Es vahr zayr goot
We enjoyed it, thank you	Es hat uns gut gefallen, danke	Es hat oons goot gefallen danker

BREAKFAST AND TEA[1]

Breakfast	Das Frühstück	Das frui-shtuik
A white coffee, please	Eine Tasse Milchkaffee bitte	Īner tasser milkh-kaffay bitter
Black coffee (with cream)	Schwarzen Kaffee (mit Sahne)	Shvartsen kaffay (mit zahner)

1. Don't forget to go into a 'Café' or 'Konditorei', particularly in Austria. To try one of the wide selection of 'Torten', a pastry speciality, with names like Sachertorte, Kaffeecremetorte, Linzertorte, Imperialtorte, will be an experience for any foreign visitor.

I would like decaffeinated coffee	Ich möchte koffeinfreien Kaffee	Ikh merkhter koffayeenfrīen kaffay
A cup of tea, please	Eine Tasse Tee bitte	Īner tasser tay bitter
I would like tea with milk/lemon	Ich möchte Tee mit Milch/Zitrone	Ikh merkhter tay mit milkh/tseetrohner
I would like a herb tea	Ich möchte einen Kräutertee	Ikh merkhter īnen kroytair-tay
May we have some sugar, please?	Können wir bitte etwas Zucker haben?	Kernen veer bitter etvas tsookair hahben
Do you have artificial sweeteners?	Haben Sie Süssstoff?	Hahben zee zuis-shtoff
Hot/cold milk	Warme/kalte Milch	Varmer/kalter milkh
Bread	Brot	Broht
A roll and butter, please	Ein Brötchen und Butter bitte	Īn brert-khen oont boottair bitter
Toast	Toast	Tohst
More butter, please	Etwas mehr Butter bitte	Etvas mayr boottair bitter
Have you some marmalade/jam/honey?	Haben Sie Orangenmarmelade/Marmelade/Honig?	Hahben zee oranjen-marmelahder/marmelahder/hohnikh
I'd like	Ich möchte	Ikh merkhter
a soft-boiled egg	ein weichgekochtes Ei	īn vīkhgekokhtes ī
a hard-boiled egg	ein hartgekochtes Ei	īn hartgekokhtes ī
fried eggs	ein Spiegelei	īn shpeegel-ī
scrambled eggs	Rührei	ruir-ī

Ham	Der Schinken	Dair shinken
Cheese	Der Käse	Dair kayzer
What fruit juices have you?	Was für Obstsäfte haben Sie?	Vas fuir ohpst-zefter hahben zee
Orange/tomato/(black, red) currant juice	Der Apfelsinensaft (Orangensaft)/ Tomatensaft/ Johannisbeersaft (schwarz, rot)	Dair apfelzeenenzaft (oranjenzaft)/ tohmahtenzaft/ johanisbairzaft (shvarts, roht)
Fresh fruit	Frisches Obst	Frishes opst
Yoghurt	Der Joghurt	Yogoort
Pastry[1]	Das Gebäck	Gebeck
Flaky/short pastry	Der Blätterteig/ Mürbeteig	Blettair-tīkh/muirber-tīkh
Tart/Layer cake	Die Torte	Torter
Cake	Der Kuchen	Kookhen
Help yourself at the buffet	*Bedienen Sie sich am Buffet	Bedeenen zee zikh am bui-fay

SNACKS AND PICNICS

| Can I have a sandwich, please? | Kann ich bitte ein belegtes Brot haben? | Kan ikh bitter īn belaygtes broht hahben |
| What are those things over there? | Was ist das dort? | Vas ist das dohrt |

1. For names of cakes and pastries see pp. 103-5

What are they made of?	Woraus ist es gemacht?	Vohrows ist es gemakht
What is in them?	Was ist da drin?	Vas ist da drin
I'll have one of those, please	Eins davon bitte	Īns dahfon bitter
It's to take away	Zum Mitnehmen	Tsoom mit-nay-men
biscuits	die Kekse	kaykzer
bread	das Brot	broht
butter	die Butter	boottair
cheese	der Käse	kayzer
chips	die Pommes frites	pom freet
chocolate bar	die Tafel Schokolade	tahfel shohkohlahder
cold cuts	der Aufschnitt	owf-shnit
egg(s)	das Ei (die Eier)	ī (īer)
ham	der Schinken	shinken
ice cream (*flavours*: p. 103)	das Eis	īs
open sandwich	das belegte Brot	belaygte broht
pancakes	der Pfannkuchen/die Palatschinke	pfankookhen/palaht-shinker
pickles	die Essigfrüchte	essikh-fruikhter
roll	das Brötchen	brertkhen
salad	der Salat	salaht
sausage (roll)	die Wurst (pastete)	voorst (pastayter)
snack	der Imbiss	imbis
snack bar	der Schnellimbiss	shnell-imbis
soup	die Suppe	zoopper

| tomato | **die Tomate** | tohmahter |
| waffles | **die Waffel** | vaffel |

DRINKS[1]

Bar	**Die Bar/die Schenke/der Ausschank**	Bahr/shenker/ows-shank
Café	**Das Café/das Kaffeehaus**	Kafay/kaffay-hows
A bottle of the local house wine, please	**Eine Flasche hiesigen Weins bitte**	Īner flasher heezigen vīns bitter
I want to see the wine list	**Ich möchte die Weinkarte sehen**	Ikh merkhter dee vīn-karter zayen
Do you serve the wine by the glass?	**Haben Sie offenen Wein?**	Hahben zee offenen vīn
Soft drinks	**Alkoholfreie Getränke**	Alkohohlfrīer getrenker
Do you serve cocktails?	**Haben Sie Cocktails?**	Hahben zee kocktails
Carafe/glass	**die Karaffe/das Glas**	Dee karaffer/das glas
Bottle/half bottle	**Die Flasche/kleine Flasche**	Dee flasher/klīner flasher
Two glasses of beer	**Zwei Gläser Bier**	Tsvī glayzair beer
Pint/half pint	**Ein grosses/kleines Bier**	Īn grohses/klīnes beer
Do you have draught beer?	**Haben Sie Bier vom Fass?**	Hahben zee beer fom fas

1. For the names of beverages see pp. 106

Light/dark beer	Helles/dunkles Bier	Helles/doonkles beer
Two more beers	Noch zwei Bier	Nokh tsvī beer
I'd like	Ich möchte	Ikh merkhter
a long soft drink with ice	einen Fruchtsaft mit Eis	īnen frookhtzaft mit īs
an apple juice	einen Apfelsaft	īnen apfelzaft
an orange juice	einen Orangensaft	īnen oranjenzaft
a fruit juice	einen Obstsaft	īnen ohpst-zaft
a milk shake	einen Milchshake	īnen milkhshayk
an iced coffee	einen Eiskaffee	īnen īs-kaffay
a hot chocolate	eine heisse Schokolade	īner hisser shoh-kohlahder
an iced tea	einen Eistee	īnen īs-tay
a China tea	einen chinesischen Tee	īnen kheenayzishen tay
Three black coffees and one with cream	Dreimal schwarzen Kaffee und einen mit Sahne	Drīmahl shvartsen kaffay oont īnen mit zahner
Tea with milk/lemon	Tee mit Milch/Zitrone	Tay mit milkh/tseetrohner
Neat/on the rocks	Pur/mit Eis	Poor/mit īs
With (soda) water	Mit (Soda) Wasser	Mit (sohdah) vassair
Mineral water	Das Mineralwasser	Minairahl-vassair
Ice cubes	Die Eiswürfel	Dee īsvuirfel
Cheers!	Prost!	Prohst
I'd like another glass of water, please	Ich möchte bitte noch ein Glas Wasser	Ikh merkhter bitter nokh īn glas vassair
The same again, please	Noch einmal dasselbe bitte	Nokh īnmahl das-selber bitter

| May we have an ashtray? | Können wir einen Aschenbecher haben? | Kernen veer īnen ashenbekhair hahben |

RESTAURANT VOCABULARY

artificial sweetener	das Süssstoff	zuis-shtof
ashtray	der Aschenbecher	ashen-bekhair
bill	die Rechnung	rekhnoong
bowl	die Schüssel	shuisel
bread	das Brot	broht
butter	die Butter	booter
cigarettes	die Zigaretten	tseegaretten
cloakroom	die Toilette	twaletter
course (dish)	der Gang	gang
cream	die Sahne	zahner
cup	die Tasse	tasser
dressing	die Salatsosse	zalaht-sohser
fork	die Gabel	gahbel
glass	das Glas	glas
headwaiter	der Oberkellner	ohberkelnair
hungry (to be)	Hunger haben/ hungrig sein	hoongair hahben/ hoongrikh zīn
knife	das Messer	messer
light (easily digested) meals	die Schonkost	shohnkost
matches	die Streichhölzer	shtrīkh-herltser

menu	die Speisekarte	shpīzerkarter
mustard	der Senf	zenf
napkin	die Serviette	zairveeyetter
oil	das Öl	erl
pepper	der Pfeffer	pfeffer
pickles	die Essigfrüchte	esikhfruikhter
plate	der Teller	tellair
restaurant	das Restaurant	restorant
salt	das Salz	salts
sauce	die Sauce	sohser
saucer	die Untertasse	oontair-tasser
service	die Bedienung	bedeenoong
spoon	der Löffel	lerffel
sugar	der Zucker	tsooker
table	der Tisch	tish
tablecloth	das Tischtuch	tishtookh
thirsty (to be)	Durst haben/durstig sein	doorst hahben/doorstikh zīn
tip	das Trinkgeld	trinkgelt
toothpick	der Zahnstocher	tsahn-shtokhair
vegetarian	der Vegetarier	vegetahree-er
vinegar	der Essig	essikh
waiter	der Kellner	kelnair
waitress	die Kellnerin	kelnairin
water	das Wasser	vassair

THE MENU

VORSPEISEN

Artischocken	artichokes
Austern	oysters
Bismarckhering	soused herring with onions
Gänseleberpastete	pâté de foie
Geräucherter Lachs	smoked salmon
Königinpastete	pastry filled with veal
Matjesfilet ('Hausfrauenart')	herring fillet (with apple and sour cream)
(Geeiste) Melone	(iced) melon
Ölsardinen (mit Brot)	tinned sardines (with bread)
Räucheraal	smoked eel
Rollmops	rollmops

Russische Eier	hard boiled eggs with caviare, capers and mayonnaise
(Westfälischer) Schinken	(raw) ham
Schinkenwurst	ham sausage
(Weinberg)schnecken	snails
Spargelspitzen	asparagus tips
Stangenspargel mit Kräutersauce	asparagus with herb sauce
Strammer Max	ryebread, raw ham and fried eggs
Wurstplatte	assorted sliced sausage

SUPPEN

Aalsuppe	eel soup
Bohnensuppe	bean soup
Erbsensuppe	pea soup
Gaisburger Marsch	vegetable soup with dumplings
Gemüsesuppe	vegetable soup
Gulaschsuppe	beef and paprika soup
Hühnerbrühe	chicken broth
Kartoffelsuppe	potato soup
Kirschkaltschale	cold cherry soup
Kraftbrühe mit Ei/Magen	bouillon with egg/tripe
Leberknödelsuppe	clear soup with liver dumplings
Linsensuppe	lentil soup
Mandelsuppe	almond and cream soup
Nudelsuppe	noodle soup

Ochsenschwanzsuppe	oxtail soup
Schildkrötensuppe	turtle soup
Tomatensuppe	tomato soup
Zwiebelsuppe	onion soup

FISCH

Aal	eel
Aal grün mit Dillsauce	fresh eel with dill sauce
Austern	oysters
Barsch	sea perch, bass
Butt	flounder
Forelle	trout
Garnele	shrimp
Hecht	pike
Heilbutt	halibut
Hering	herring
Hummer	lobster
Kabeljau	cod
Karpfen	carp
Krabben	small shrimps
Krebs	crab
Lachs, Salm	salmon
Makrele	mackerel
Muscheln	mussels
Rotbarsch	redfish

Sardellen	anchovies
Schellfisch	haddock
Scholle	plaice
Seebarsch	bass
Seezunge	sole
Steinbutt	turbot
Thunfisch	tunny
Zander	pike-perch

FLEISCH

Kalb:	veal:
Kalbsbrust	breast of veal
Kalbshaxe	roast knuckle of veal
Kalbskoteletts	veal cutlets, chops
Kalbsvögel	veal roulade
(Wiener) Schnitzel	(fried) escalope of veal
Lamm/Hammel:	lamb/mutton:
Hammelbraten/Lammbraten	roast mutton/lamb
Lammskeule	roast leg of lamb
Hammelragout	mutton stew
Rind:	beef:
Beefsteak	steak
Deutsches Beefsteak	minced beef, hamburger
Gekochte Rinderbrust	boiled brisket of beef
Gulasch	goulash

Rinderbraten	roast beef
Rinderfilet	fillet of beef
Rindsrouladen	beef olives
Rinderschmorbraten	braised beef
Sauerbraten	braised pickled beef
Schweinefleisch:	pork:
(Kasseler) Rippchen	(smoked) pork chop
Schweinebraten	roast pork
Schweinefilet	loin of pork
Eisbein	pickled pork knuckle
Spanferkel	sucking pig

WURST UND INNEREIEN

Blutwurst	black pudding
Bockwurst	large boiling sausage
Bratwurst	frying sausage
Knackwurst	frankfurter
Kochwurst	cold cuts
Nürnberger Würstchen	small spiced chipolatas
Pinkel	smoked sausage with onions
Weisswurst	veal sausage
Flecke	tripe
Fleischkloss	meatball
Frikadelle	rissole, croquette
Hirn	brain

Kalbsbries (*North German:* **Kalbsmilcher**)	sweetbreads
Leber	liver
Nieren	kidneys
Ochsenschwanz	oxtail
Schinken	ham (smoked raw)
Gekochter Schinken	cooked ham
Schlachtplatte	mixed cold meat
Speck	bacon
Zunge	tongue

WILD UND GEFLÜGEL

Ente	duck
Fasan	pheasant
Gans	goose
Hähnchen/Huhn	chicken
am Spiess	roast
Flügel	wing
Brust	breast
Hase	hare
Hasenpfeffer	jugged hare
(Gespickter) Hirsch	(larded) deer
Huhn	chicken
Kaninchen	rabbit
Rebhuhn	partridge

Reh(braten)	(roast) venison
Rehrücken	saddle of deer
Taube	pigeon
Truthahn/Pute	turkey

GEMÜSE UDN SALAT

Blumenkohl	cauliflower
Bohnen	beans
Grüne Bohnen	green beans
Stangenbohnen	runner beans
Weisse Bohnen	haricot beans
Brunnenkresse	watercress
Champignons	mushrooms
Edelpilze	(best varieties of) wild mushrooms
Erbsen	peas
Grüner Salat	lettuce
Grünkohl	kale
Gurke	cucumber
Gewürzgurken	pickled cucumbers
Himmel und Erde	potato and apple
Kartoffeln	potatoes
Salzkartoffeln	boiled potatoes
Kartoffelpüree	mashed potatoes
Kartoffelklösse	potato dumplings
Pommes frites	chips

Bratkartoffeln	fried potatoes
Rösti	grated, fried potatoes
Kartoffelsalat	potato salad
Kastanien	chestnuts
Knoblauch	garlic
Kohl (Weiss-, Rot-)	cabbage (white, red)
Kopfsalat	(cabbage) lettuce
Kürbis	pumpkin/marrow
Lauch, Porree	leeks
Meerrettich	horse radish
Paprika (-schoten)	peppers
Pfifferlinge	mushrooms (*chanterelles*)
Pilze	mushrooms
Reis	rice
Rettich	radish
Rosenkohl	brussels sprouts
Rösti	grated, fried potatoes
Rote Beete	beetroots
Rüben	swedes
Salat	lettuce/salad
Sauerampfer	sorrel
Sauerkraut	pickled cabbage
Schwarzwurzeln	scorzonera
Sellerie	celery
Spargel	asparagus
Spinat	spinach

Steinpilze	mushrooms (*Boletus edulis, cèpes*)
Tomaten	tomatoes
Weisse Rübe	turnip
Wirsingkohl	savoy cabbage
Wurzeln (Möhren, Karotten)	carrots
Zwiebeln	onions

KNÖDEL

Leberknödel	liver dumplings
Kartoffelknödel	potato dumplings
Klösse	dumplings
Kräuterklösse	herb dumplings
Maultasche	Swabian ravioli
Nockerl	dumpling
Nudeln	noodles
Spätzle	small noodles

EIER

Gekochtes Ei (weich/hart)	boiled egg (soft/hard)
Omelett	omelette
mit Pilzen	with mushrooms
mit Kräutern	with herbs
Bauernomelett	with diced bacon and onion

Rührei	scrambled eggs
Russische Eier	hard boiled eggs with caviare, capers and mayonnaise
Spiegeleier	fried eggs
Verlorene Eier	poached eggs

KÄSE

Allgäuer, Emmentaler	Swiss cheese
Käseteller	cheese board
Kümmelkäse	cheese with caraway seed
Rahmkäse, Sahnekäse	cream cheese
Räucherkäse	smoked cheese
Schmelzkäse	cheese spread
Thüringer Käse, Harzkäse	sausage-shaped cheeses made from curd

NACHSPEISEN UND KUCHEN

Apfelkuchen	apple cake
Apfelstrudel	flaky pastry stuffed with apple, walnut, spices
Auflauf	soufflé
Eis (Speiseeis):	ice cream:
Erdbeer-	strawberry
Gemischtes-	mixed

Mokka-	coffee
Nuss-	nut
Schokoladen-	chocolate
Vanille-	vanilla
Eisbecher	ice cream with fresh fruit
Frisches Obst	fresh fruit
Fruchttörtchen	small fruit tart
Kaiserschmarren	shredded pancake with raisins and syrup
Käsetorte	cheesecake
Keks	biscuit
Krapfen	doughnuts
Kuchen	cake
Lebkuchen	spiced cake, gingerbread
Linzertorte	cake spread with ground almonds and jam, topped with whipped cream
Makronen	macaroons
Mohrenkopf	pastry filled with cream, topped with chocolate
Mokkatorte	coffee cake
Nusstorte	nut cake
Obstkompott	stewed fruit
Obstkuchen	fruit tart
Obstsalat	fruit salad
Palatschinke	pancake filled either with sausage or with cheese and nuts or with jam

Pfannkuchen	pancakes, doughnuts, fritters
Pfirsich Melba	peach melba
Pflaumenkuchen	plum cake
Rote Grütze	raspberries or redcurrants cooked with semolina, served with cream
Sachertorte	chocolate cake spread with jam and chocolate icing
Sandtorte	madeira cake
Schlagsahne	whipped cream
Stollen	rich cake with fruit and nuts
Streuselkuchen	cake sprinkled with almonds and cinnamon butter
Torte	tart, flat cake

OBST UND NÜSSE

Ananas	pineapple
Apfel	apple
Apfelsine	orange
Aprikose	apricot
Banane	banana
Birne	pear
Brombeere	blackberry
Erdbeere	strawberry
Feige	fig
Haselnuss	hazelnut
Himbeere	raspberry

Johannisbeere (rot)	redcurrant
Johannisbeere (schwarz)	blackcurrant
Kirsche	cherry
Mandarine	mandarin orange, tangerine
Mandel	almond
Melone	melon
Pampelmuse	grapefruit
Pfirsich	peach
Pflaume	plum
Reineclaude	greengage
Stachelbeere	gooseberry
(Wein)traube	grape
Walnuss	walnut
Wassermelone	water melon
Zitrone	lemon
Zwetsche	damson

GETRÄNKE

Alkohol	alcohol
Apfelsaft	apple juice
Apfelsinensaft	orange juice
Apfelwein	cider
Bier (hell/dunkel)	beer (light/dark)
Bier vom Fass	draught beer
Bockbier	bock beer (dark and very strong)

Bowle	fruit cup
Cognac	brandy
(Himbeer)geist	(raspberry) eau-de-vie
Glühwein	mulled wine
Grog	grog
Heisse Schokolade	hot chocolate
Kaffee	coffee
Milchkaffee	white
Schwarzer	black
Mit Sahne	with cream
Kaffee Haag (ohne Caffein)	(caffeine free)
Kräutertee	herb tea
Hagebutten	rose hip
Kamille	camomile
Lindenblüten	lime
Pfefferminz	mint
Likör	liqueur
Limonade	lemonade
Märzen	strong beer
Milch	milk
Mineralwasser	mineral water
Obstsaft	fruit juice
Orangeade	orangeade
Orangensaft	orange juice
Pilsener	lager
Portwein	port

Rum	rum
Sekt	German sparkling wine
Schnaps	German grain spirit
Sherry	sherry
Sodawasser	soda water
Tee	tea
Tomatensaft	tomato juice
Wasser	water
(Kirsch-/Zwetschen-) Wasser	(cherry/plum) brandy
Wein	wine
Offen	open/by the glass
Rot	red
Weiss	white
Süss	sweet
Trocken	dry
Weintraubensaft	grape juice
Weinbrand	brandy
Wermut	vermouth
Whisky	whisky

SOME COOKING METHODS AND SAUCES

Fleisch	meat -
rot	rare
halbdurch	medium

durchgebraten	well-done
blau	au bleu
gebacken	baked
gebraten	roast
(in der Pfanne) gebraten	fried
gedämpft	steamed, stewed
gefüllt	stuffed
gegrillt	grilled
gekocht	boiled
geräuchert	smoked
gerieben	grated
geschmort	braised, stewed
geschwenkt	sautéed
mariniert	marinated
... püree	creamed ...
roh	raw
butter-	buttered ...
grüne Sauce	mayonnaise (or vinaigrette with chopped egg) with mixed green herbs
holländisch	with mayonnaise
Holstein	topped with fried egg, garnished with anchovy (the grand version with assorted seafood)
nach Jägerart	sautéed with mushrooms, in wine sauce
Kräuter(butter)	herb (butter)

Petersilien-	parsleyed ...
Sahne-/Rahm-	... and cream
Senf-	mustard ...
Sülz-	... in aspic

SHOPPING[1] & SERVICES

WHERE TO GO

Which is the best ...?	**Welches ist der/die/ das beste ...?**	Velkhes ist dair/dee/das bester
Where is the nearest ...?	**Wo ist der/die/das nächste ...?**	Voh ist dair/dee/das naikhster
Can you recommend a ...?	**Können Sie einen/ eine/ein ... empfehlen?**	Kernen zee īnen/īner/īn ... empfaylen

1. Shopping hours in Germany vary in different parts of the country and between large and small towns and villages; generally, however, shops open at 8 a.m. and close at 6.30 p.m., with some shops closing at lunchtime. They are closed on Sundays and public holidays (p. 197) and on Saturday afternoons, except for one Saturday a month, 'der lange Samstag', when they stay open all day. In Austria most shops are open from 8 a.m. to 12 noon and from 2 to 6 p.m. and are closed either Wednesday or Saturday afternoon. In Switzerland shops are open from 8 a.m. to 12 noon and from 2 to 6 p.m., closed Saturday afternoons.

Where is the market?	Wo ist der Markt?	Voh ist dair markt
Is there a market every day?	Ist jeden Tag Markt?	Ist yayden tahg markt?
Where can I buy ...?	Wo kann ich ... kaufen?	Voh kan ikh ... kowfen
When are the shops open?	Wann sind die Geschäfte geöffnet?	Van zint dee geshefter ge-erfnet

SHOPS AND SERVICES

antique shop	der Antiquitätenladen	anteekveetayten-lahden
baker	der Bäcker/die Bäckerei	becker/beckerī
bank	die Bank	bank
barber (see p. 129)	der Friseur	freezer
bookshop	die Buchhandlung	bookh-handloong
builder	der Bauherr	bowhair
butcher (see pp. 97-100 and 127)	die Metzgerei/die Schlachterei	Metsgerī/shlakhterī
cake shop	die Konditorei	kondeetohrī
camera shop	das Photogeschäft	fohtoh-gesheft
camping equipment	die Campingausrüstung	kampingowsruis-toong

chemist (see pp. 121-4)	die Apotheke (*for medicines*)/die Drogerie (*for cosmetics, etc.*)	apohtayker/drohgairee
confectioner (see pp. 103-5)	die Konditorei	kondeetorī
decorator	der Maler	mahlair
dentist	der Zahnarzt	tsahnartst
department store (see pp. 115-21)	das Warenhaus	vahrenhows
doctor	der Arzt	artst
dry cleaner (see p. 132)	die (chemische) Reinigung	(kaymisher) rīnigoong
electrician	der Elektriker	aylektreekair
electrical appliances	die elektrischen Geräte	aylektreeshen gayrayter
fishmonger (see p. 96)	die Fischhandlung	fish-handloong
florist	das Blumengeschäft	bloomen-gesheft
greengrocer (see pp. 100 and 105)	die Gemüsehandlung	gemuizer-handloong
grocer (see pp. 102)	das Lebensmittel-geschäft	laybensmittel-gesheft
hairdresser (see p. 129)	der (Damen)friseur	(dahmen)freezer
hardware store (see p. 131)	die Eisenwaren-handlung	īzenvahren-handloong
hypermarket	der grosse Supermarkt	grohsser zoopairmarkt
ironmonger	die Eisenwarenhandlung	īzenvahren-handloong

jeweller (see p. 141)	der Juwelier	yooveleer
launderette	die Schnellwäscherei	shnel-vesherī
laundry (see p. 132)	die Wäscherei	vesherī
liquor/wine store (see p. 106)	die Spirituosen-/ Weinhandlung	spee-ree-too-oh-zen/ vīn-handloong
market	der Markt	markt
newsagent (see p. 134)	das Zeitungsgeschäft	tsītoongs-gesheft
notary	der Notar	nohtahr
optician (see p. 136)	der Optiker	opteekair
pastry shop	die Bäckerei	bekerī
photographer	der Photograph	fohtohgrahf
plumber	der Installateur	installahter
police	die Polizei	pohleetsī
post office	die Post	post
shoemaker	der Schuster	shoostair
sports shop	das Sportgeschäft	shport-gesheft
stationer (see p. 134)	das Schreibwarengeschäft	shrīpvahren-gesheft
supermarket	der Supermarkt	zoopair-markt
sweet shop	die Süsswarenhandlung	zuissvahren-handloong
tobacconist (see p. 139)	der Tabakladen	taback-lahden
toy shop	das Spielwarengeschäft	shpeelvahren-gesheft
travel agent	das Reisebüro	rīzer-buiroh
wine merchant	die Weinhandlung	vīn-handloong

IN THE SHOP

Self-service	*Selbstbedienung	Zelpst-bedeenoong
Sale (clearance)	*Schlussverkauf/ Ausverkauf	Shloossfairkowf/ owsfairkowf
Special offer	*Sonderangebot	Zonder-angeboht
Cash desk	*Kasse	Kasser
Shop assistant	Der Verkäufer/die Verkäuferin	Fairkoyfer/fairkoyfairin
Manager	Der Geschäftsführer	Geshefts-fuirer
Can I help you?	*Was darf es sein?	Vas darf es zīn
I want to buy ...	Ich möchte ... kaufen	Ikh merkhter ... kowfen
Do you sell ...?	Verkaufen Sie ...?	Fairkowfen zee
I'm just looking round	Ich möchte mich nur umsehen	Ikh merkhter mikh noor oomzayen
I don't want to buy anything now	Ich möchte im Augenblick nichts kaufen	Ikh merkhter im owgenblik nikhts kowfen
Could you show me ...?	Könnten Sie mir bitte ... zeigen?	Kernten zee meer bitter tsīgen
We do not have that	*Das haben wir leider nicht	Das hahben veer līdair nikht
You'll find them at that counter	*Sie sind dort auf dem Verkaufstisch	Zee zint dort owf daym fairkowfs-tish
We've sold out, but we'll have more tomorrow	*Wir sind im Augenblick ausverkauft, aber morgen haben wir mehr	Veer zint im owgenblik owsfairkowft ahbair morgen hahben veer mayr

Anything else?	*Sonst noch etwas?	Zonst nokh etvas
That will be all	Das ist alles	Das ist alles
Will you take it with you?	*Möchten Sie es mitnehmen?	Merkhten zee es mitnaymen
I will take it with me	Ich nehme es gleich mit	Ikh naymer es glīkh mit
Please send them to this address/... hotel	Bitte schicken Sie es an diese Adresse/ ins Hotel ...	Bitter shicken zee es an deezer adresser/ins hohtel

CHOOSING

I want something in leather/green	Ich möchte etwas aus Leder/in grün	Ikh merkhter etvas ows laydair/in gruin
I need it to match this	Es soll hierzu passen	Es zol heer-tsoo passen
I like the one in the window	Das im Fenster gefällt mir	Das im fenstair gefellt meer
Could I see that one, please?	Darf ich das mal sehen, bitte?	Darf ikh das mahl zayen bitter
I like the colour but not the style	Mir gefällt die Farbe, aber nicht der Schnitt	Meer gefellt dee farber ahbair nikht dair shnit
I want a darker/lighter shade	Ich möchte einen dunkleren/helleren Farbton	Ikh merkhter īnen doonklairen/hellairen farbtohn
I need something warmer/thinner	Ich brauche etwas Wärmeres/ Dünneres	Ikh browkher etvas vermaires/duinnaires

Do you have one in another colour/size?	**Haben Sie es in einer anderen Farbe/ Grösse?**	Hahben zee es in īnair andairen farber/ grerser
Have you anything better/cheaper?	**Haben Sie etwas Besseres/ Billigeres?**	Hahben zee etvas bessaires/billigaires
How much is this?	**Was kostet das?**	Vas kostet das
That is too much for me	**Das ist mir zu teuer**	Das ist meer tsoo **toy**-er
What size is this?	**Welche Grösse ist das?**	Velkher grerser ist das
I take size ...[1]	**Ich brauche Grösse ...**	Ikh browkher grerser
The English/American size is ...	**Die englische/ amerikanische Grösse ist ...**	Dee englisher/ amaireekahnisher grerser ist
My collar/chest/waist is ...	**Meine Kragenweite/ mein Brustumfang/ meine Taillenweite ist ...**	Mīner krahgenvīter/mīn broostoomfung/mīner tīl-yen-vīter ist
Can I try it on?	**Kann ich es anprobieren?**	Kan ikh es anprohbeeren
It's too short/long/ tight/loose	**Es ist zu kurz/lang/ eng/weit**	Es ist tsoo koorts/lang/ eng/vīt
Have you a larger/ smaller one?	**Haben Sie ein grösseres/ kleineres?**	Hahben zee īn grerseres/klīneres
Is there a mirror?	**Ist hier ein Spiegel?**	Ist heer īn shpeegel

1. See table (p. 126) for continental sizes.

Is it colourfast?	Ist es farbecht?	Ist es farb-ekht
Is it machine-washable?	Kann es mit der Maschine gewaschen werden?	Kan es mit dair mahsheener gevashen vairden
Will it shrink?	Läuft es ein?	Loyft es īn
Is it handmade?	Ist es Handarbeit?	Ist es hantahrbīt
What's it made of?	Woraus ist es gemacht?	Vohrows ist es gemakht

MATERIALS

cotton	die Baumwolle	dee bowmvoller
lace	die Spitze	dee shpitser
leather	das Leder	das laydair
linen	das Leinen	das līnen
plastic	der Kunststoff	dair koonst-shtoff
silk	die Seide	dee zīder
suede	das Wildleder	das viltlaydair
synthetic	die Synthetik	dee zuintayteek
wool	die Wolle	dee voller

COLOURS

| beige | beige | behj |
| black | schwarz | shvarts |

blue	**blau**	blow
brown	**braun**	brown
gold	**golden**	golden
green	**grün**	gruin
grey	**grau**	grow
mauve	**lila**	leelah
orange	**orangenfarbig**	oranjenfarbikh
pink	**rosa**	rozah
purple	**purpur**	poorpoor
red	**rot**	roht
silver	**silbern**	zilbairn
white	**weiss**	vīs
yellow	**gelb**	gelp

COMPLAINTS

I want to see the manager	**Ich möchte den Geschäftsführer sprechen**	Ikh merkhter dayn geshefts-fuirer shprekhen
I bought this yesterday	**Ich habe dies gestern gekauft**	Ikh hahber dees gestairn gekowft
It doesn't work/fit	**Es funktioniert/passt nicht**	Es foonktsyoneert/passt nikht
This is	**Es ist**	Es ist
dirty	**schmutzig**	shmootsikh
torn	**zerrissen**	tsairissen
broken	**kaputt**	kahpoot
bad	**schlecht**	shlekht

This is stained/cracked	Es hat Flecken/einen Sprung	Es hat fleken/īnen shproong
Will you change it, please?	Können Sie es bitte umtauschen?	Kernen zee es bitter oomtowshen
Will you refund my money?	Können Sie mir bitte mein Geld zurückgeben?	Kernen zee meer bitter mīn gelt tsooruik-gayben
Here is the receipt	Hier ist die Quittung	Heer ist dee kvitoong

PAYING

How much is this?	Wie teuer ist das?	Vee toyer ist das
That's ... DM, please	*Das macht ... Mark bitte	Das makht ... mark bitter
They are ... DM each	*Sie kosten ... Mark pro Stück	Zee kosten ... mark pro stuik
How much does that come to?	Was macht das?	Vas makht das
That will be ...	*Das macht ...	Das makht
Will you take English/American currency?	Nehmen Sie englisches/amerikanisches Geld?	Naymen zee englishes/amaireekahnishes gelt
Do you take credit cards/travellers' cheques?	Nehmen Sie Kreditkarten/Reiseschecks?	Naymen zee kraydeet-karten/rīzer-sheks

Do I have to pay VAT?	Muss ich Mehrwertsteuer zahlen?	Moos ikh mayr-vert-shtoyer tsahlen
Please pay the cashier	*Bitte, zahlen Sie an der Kasse	Bitter tsahlen zee an dair kasser
May I have a receipt, please?	Kann ich bitte eine Quittung haben?	Kan ikh bitter īner kvitoong hahben
You've given me too little/too much change	Sie haben mir zu wenig/zu viel Geld herausgegeben	Zee hahben meer tsoo vaynikh/tsoo feel gelt hairows-gegayben

CHEMIST[1]

Can you prepare this prescription for me, please?	Können Sie bitte dieses Rezept für mich zubereiten?	Kernen zee bitter deezes raytsept fuir mikh tsooberīten
Have you a small first-aid kit?	Haben Sie einen kleinen Verbandskasten?	Hahben zee īnen klīnen fairbants-kasten
I want some aspirin/sun cream (for children)	Ich möchte Aspirin/Sonnencreme (für Kinder)	Ikh merkhter aspireen/zonnenkraymer (fuir kindair)
A packet of adhesive plaster	Eine Schachtel Hansaplast/Heftpflaster	Īner shakhtel hanzah-plast/heftpflastair

1. You go to an **Apotheke** for prescriptions, medicines, etc., and to a **Drogerie** for toilet requisites. (See also AT THE DOCTOR'S, p. 173.)

I want	Ich möchte	Ikh merkhter
an antiseptic cream	eine antiseptische Creme	īner anteezepteesher kraymer
a disinfectant	etwas zum Desinfizieren	etvas tsoom desinfeetseeren
a mouthwash	ein Mundspülmittel	īn moontshpuilmittel
some nose drops	Nasentropfen	nahzentropfen
Can you give me something for constipation? diarrhoea? indigestion?	Haben Sie etwas gegen Verstopfung? Durchfall? Magenverstimmung?	Hahben zee etvas gaygen fairshtopfoong doorkhfall mahgenfairshtimmoong
Do you sell contraceptives?	Verkaufen Sie empfängnisverhütende Mittel?	Fairkowfen zee empfengnisfairhuitender mittel
I want something for insect bites	Ich möchte etwas gegen Insektenstiche	Ikh merkhter etvas gaygen inzekten shtikher
Can you give me something for sunburn?	Können Sie mir etwas gegen Sonnenbrand geben?	Kernen zee meer etvas gaygen zonnenbrant gayben
I want some throat lozenges/stomach pills	Ich brauche Halspastillen/ Magentabletten	Ikh browkher halspastillen/ mahgentabletten
Do you have sanitary towels? tampons? cotton wool?	Haben Sie Binden? Tampons? Watte?	Hahben zee binden tampons vatter

| I need something for a hangover/travel sickness | Ich brauche etwas für einen Kater/ Reiseübelkeit | Ikh browkher etvas fuir īnen kahtair/rīzer- uibelkīt |

TOILET ARTICLES[1]

A packet of razor blades, please	Eine Schachtel Rasierklingen bitte	Īner shakhtel rahzeerklingen bitter
How much is this after-shave lotion?	Wie teuer ist dieses Rasierwasser?	Vee toyair ist deezes rahzeer-vassair
A tube of toothpaste, please	Eine Tube Zahnpasta bitte	Īner toober tsahnpasta bitter
A box of paper handkerchiefs/a roll of toilet paper, please	Eine Schachtel Papiertaschentücher/ eine Rolle Toilettenpapier, bitte	Īner shakhtel papeer- tashentuikher/īner roller twaletten-papeer bitter
I want some eau-de-cologne/perfume/ cream	Ich möchte Kölnisch Wasser/Parfüm/ Creme	Ikh merkhter kerlnish vassair/parfuim/ kraymer
May I try it?	Kann ich es ausprobieren?	Kan ikh es owsprohbeeren
What kinds of toilet soap have you?	Welche Arten von Seife haben Sie?	Velkher arten fon zīfer hahben zee

1. You go to an **Apotheke** for prescriptions, medicines, etc., and to a **Drogerie** for toilet articles.

A bottle/tube of shampoo, for dry/greasy hair	Eine Flasche/Tube Schampoo für trockenes/fettiges Haar	īner flasher/toober shampoh fuir trokenes/fettiges hahr
Do you have any suntan oil/cream?	Haben Sie Sonnenöl/Sonnencreme?	Hahben zee zonnenerl/zonnenkraymer
I'd like	Ich möchte	Ikh merkhter
some cleansing cream/lotion	eine Reinigungscreme/Lotion	īner rīneegoongs-kraymer/lohtsyohn
a hair conditioner	eine Pflegespülung	īner pflayger-shpuiloong
a hand cream	eine Handcreme	īner hantkraymer
some lipsalve	einen Lippenpflegestift	īnen lippen-pflayger-shtift
a moisturizer	eine Feuchtigkeitscreme	īner foykhtikh-kītskraymer

CLOTHES AND SHOES[1]

I want a hat/sunhat	Ich möchte einen Hut/Sonnenhut	Ikh merkhter īnen hoot/zonnenhoot
Where are beach clothes?	Wo finde ich Strandkleidung?	Voh finder ikh shtrantklīdoong
I want a short/long sleeved shirt, collar size ...	Ich möchte ein Hemd mit kurzen/langen Ärmeln, Kragenweite ...	Ikh merkhter īn hemt mit koortsen/langen ermeln krahgenvīter

1. For sizes see p. 126

Where can I find socks/stockings?	Wo finde ich Socken/Strümpfe?	Voh finder ikh zocken/ shtruimpfer
I am looking for a blouse a bra a dress a sweater	Ich suche eine Bluse einen BH ein Kleid einen Pullover	Ikh zookher īner bloozer īnen bayhah īn klīt īnen poollovair
I need a coat a raincoat a jacket	Ich brauche einen Mantel einen Regenmantel eine Jacke	Ikh browkher īnen mantel īnen raygenmantel īner yakker
Do you sell buttons? elastic? zips?	Verkaufen Sie Knöpfe? Gummiband? Reissverschlüsse?	Fairkowfen zee knerpfe goomibant rīsfairshluisser
I need a pair of walking shoes beach sandals black shoes	Ich brauche ein Paar Strassenschuhe Strandsandalen schwarze Schuhe	Ikh browkher īn pahr shtrahssen-shooer shtrant-zandahlen shvartser shooer
This doesn't fit	Dies passt nicht	Dees passt nikht
I don't know the German size	Ich weiss die deutsche Grösse nicht	Ikh vīs dee doytsher grerser nikht
Can you measure me?	Können Sie mich messen?	Kernen zee mikh messen
It's for a 3-year-old	Es ist für eine(n) Dreijährige(n)	Es ist fuir īner(n) drīyayreeger(n)
These heels are too high/too low	Diese Absätze sind zu hoch/zu niedrig	Deezer apzetser zint tsoo hohkh/tsoo needrikh

CLOTHING SIZES

WOMEN'S DRESSES, ETC.

American	8	10	12	14	16	18
British	10	12	14	16	18	20
German	36	38	40	42	44	46

MEN'S PULLOVERS, ETC.

British and American	36	38	40	42	44	46
Continental	46	48	50	52	54	56

MEN'S SHIRTS

British and American	13	$13\frac{1}{2}$	14	$14\frac{1}{2}$	15	$15\frac{1}{2}$	$15\frac{3}{4}$	16	$16\frac{1}{2}$	17	$17\frac{1}{2}$
Continental	34	35	36	37	38	39	40	41	42	43	44

WAIST, CHEST/BUST AND HIPS

Inches	28	30	32	34	36	38	40
Centimetres	71	76	81	87	92	97	102
Inches	42	44	46	48	50	52	54
Centimetres	107	112	117	122	127	132	137

MEN'S SOCKS

British and American	10	$10\frac{1}{2}$	11	$11\frac{1}{2}$	12
Continental	39–40	41–42	43–44	45–46	47–48

STOCKINGS

British and American	8	8½	9	9½	10	10½	11
Continental	0	1	2	3	4	5	6

SHOES

British	1	2	3	4	5	6	7	8	9	10	11	12
American	2½	3½	4½	5½	6½	7½	8½	9½	10½	11½	12½	13½
Continental	33	34–5	36	37	38	39–40	41	42	43	44	45	46

FOOD[1]

Give me a kilo/half a kilo (pound) of ...	**Geben Sie mir ein Kilo/ein halbes Kilo (ein Pfund) ...**	Gayben zee meer īn kee-loh/īn halbes kee-loh (īn pfoont)
I want some sweets/ chocolates, please	**Ich möchte bitte Bonbons/Pralinen**	Ikh merkhter bitter bongbongs/praleenen
A bottle of milk/wine/ beer, please	**Eine Flasche Milch/ Wein/Bier bitte**	Īner flasher milkh/vīn/ beer bitter
I want a jar/can/packet of ...	**Ich möchte ein Glas/eine Dose/ein Paket ...**	Ikh merkhter īn glas/īner dohser/īn pakayt
I want a jar/can/packet of ...	**Ich möchte ein Glas/eine Dose/ein Paket ...**	Ikh merkhter īn glas/īner dohser/īn pakayt

1. See also the various MENU sections (pp. 94-108) and WEIGHTS AND MEASURES (pp. 201-4).

... slices of ham please	... Scheiben Schinken bitte	... shīben shinken bitter
A loaf of bread	Ein Brot	Īn broht
Dark rye bread	Vollkornbrot/ Schwarzbrot	Follkornbroht/ shvartsbroht
Is it fresh or frozen?	Ist es frisch oder gefroren?	Ist es frish ohdair gefrohren
Do you sell frozen foods?	Verkaufen Sie Tiefkühlkost?	Fairkowfen zee teefkuilkost
These pears are too hard/soft	Diese Birnen sind zu hart/weich	Deezer birnen zint tsoo hart/vīkh
Is it fresh?	Ist es frisch?	Ist es frish
Are they ripe?	Sind sie reif?	Zint zee rīf
This is bad/stale	Dies ist schlecht/alt	Dees ist shlekht/alt
Will you mince it?	Würden Sie es durch den Fleischwolf drehen?	Vuirden zee es doorkh dayn flīshvolf drayen
Will you clean the fish?	Können Sie den Fisch sauber machen?	Kernen zee dayn fish zowbair makhen
Leave/take off the head	Lassen Sie den Kopf dran/nehmen Sie den Kopf ab	Lassen zee dayn kopf dran/naymen zee dayn kopf ap
Please fillet the fish	Würden Sie den Fisch bitte filetieren	Vuirden zee dayn fish bitter feelayteeren
Shall I help myself?	Soll ich mich selbst bedienen?	Zoll ikh mikh zelpst bedeenen

HAIRDRESSER AND BARBER

May I make an appointment for this morning/tomorrow afternoon?	Kann ich mich für heute morgen/ morgen nachmittag anmelden?	Kan ikh mikh fuir hoyter morgen/morgen nakhmittahg anmelden
What time?	Zu welcher Zeit?	Tsoo velkhair tsīt
I want my hair cut	Ich möchte mir die Haare schneiden lassen	Ikh merkhter meer dee hahrer shnīden lassen
I want my hair trimmed just a little	Bitte schneiden Sie mir das Haar nur etwas nach	Bitter shnīden zee meer das hahr noor etvas nahkh
Shorter on top	Oben kürzer	Ohben kuirtsair
Not too short at the sides	Nicht zu kurz an den Seiten	Nikht tsoo koorts an dayn zīten
I'll have it shorter at the back, please	Hinten möchte ich es bitte kürzer haben	Hinten merkhter ikh es bitter kuirtsair hahben
No shorter	Nicht kürzer	Nikht kuirtsair
That's fine	Das ist gut so	Das ist goot zoh
My hair is oily/dry	Mein Haar ist fettig/trocken	Mīn hahr ist fettikh/ trocken
I want a shampoo	Waschen bitte	Vashen bitter
Please use conditioner	Bitte geben Sie mir eine Pflegespülung	Bitter gayben zee meer īner pflayger-shpuiloong

I want my hair washed, styled and blow-dried	Waschen, legen und trockenföhnen bitte	Vashen laygen oont trockenfernen bitter
I want a colour rinse	Ich möchte einen Farbfestiger	Ikh merkhter īnen farbfestigair
Please do not use any hairspray	Bitte benutzen Sie keinen Haarspray	Bitter benootsen zee kīnen hahrspray
I want a perm	Ich möchte eine Dauerwelle	Ikh merkhter īner dowairveller
I want a colour rinse	Ich möchte einen Farbfestiger	Ikh merkhter īnen farbfestigair
I'd like to see a colour chart	Kann ich bitte eine Farbskala sehen?	Kan ikh bitter īner farbskahlah zayen
I want a darker/lighter shade	Ich möchte einen dunkleren/helleren Farbton	Ikh merkhter īnen doonkleren/helleren farbtohn
I'd like it set this way, please	Ich möchte es bitte so gelegt haben	Ikh merkhter es bitter zoh gelaygt hahben
The water is too cold	Das Wasser ist zu kalt	Das vassair ist tsoo kalt
The dryer is too hot	Die Trockenhaube ist zu heiss	Dee trocken-howber ist tsoo hīs
Thank you, I like it very much	Danke, so gefällt es mir gut	Danker zoh gefelt es meer goot
I want a shave/manicure	Ich möchte mich rasieren/maniküren lassen	Ikh merkhter mikh razeeren/manikuiren lassen
Please trim my beard/moustache	Bitte stutzen Sie den Bart/den Schnurrbart	Bitter shtoo-tsen zee dayn bahrt/dayn schnoor-bahrt

HARDWARE[1]

Where is the camping equipment?	Wo ist die Camping/Zelt Ausrüstung?	Voh ist dee **kamping/tselt** owsruistoong
Do you have a battery for this?	Haben Sie hierfür eine Batterie?	**Hahben** zee heerfuir **ī**ner batteree
Where can I get butane gas/paraffin?	Wo kann ich Butangas/ Petroleum bekommen?	Voh kan ikh **boo**tahngas/ **pay**trohlayoom bekommen
I need a bottle-opener can-opener corkscrew	Ich brauche einen Flaschenöffner Dosenöffner Korkenzieher	Ikh **brow**kher **ī**nen **flashen**-erfnair **dohzen**-erfnair **korken**-tseeair
I'd like some candles/ matches	Ich möchte Kerzen/ Streichhölzer	Ikh **merkh**ter **kert**sen/ **shtrī**kh-herltsair
I want a flashlight a (pen) knife	Ich möchte eine Taschenlampe ein (Taschen) Messer	Ikh **merkh**ter **ī**ner tashen-lamper **ī**n (tashen)messair
a pair of scissors	eine Schere	**ī**ner shayrer
Do you sell string/ rope?	Verkaufen Sie Band/Tau?	**Fair**kowfen zee bant/tow
Where can I find washing-up liquid? scouring powder? soap pads?	Wo finde ich Abwaschseife? Scheuersand? Seifenkissen?	Voh **finder** ikh **ap**vashzīfer **shoy**airsant **zī**fenkissen

1. See also CAMPING, p. 67.

Do you have a dishcloth/brush?	Haben Sie ein Geschirrtuch/eine Bürste?	Hahben zee in geshirtookh/iner buirtser
I need	Ich brauche	Ikh browkher
a groundsheet	eine Zeltbahn	iner tseltbahn
a bucket	einen Eimer	inen imair
a frying pan	eine Bratpfanne	iner brahtpfanner

LAUNDRY AND DRY CLEANING

Where is the nearest launderette/dry cleaner?	Wo ist die nächste Schnellwäscherei/Reinigung?	Voh ist dee naikhster shnellveshairi/rineegoong
I want to have these things washed/cleaned	Ich möchte diese Sachen waschen lassen/reinigen lassen	Ikh merkhter deezer zakhen vashen lassen/rinigen lassen
These stains won't come out	*Diese Flecken gehen nicht raus	Deezer fleken gayen nikht rows
Can you get this stain out?	Können Sie diesen Flecken rausmachen?	Kernen zee deezen fleken rowsmakhen
It is	Es ist	Es ist
coffee	Kaffee	kaffay
wine	Wein	vin
grease	Fett	fett
When will they be ready?	Wann sind sie fertig?	Van zint zee fairtikh
It only needs to be pressed	Es muss nur geplättet (gebügelt) werden	Es moos noor gepletet (gebuigelt) vairden

This is torn; can you mend it?	Dies ist zerrissen; können Sie es ausbessern?	Dees ist tserissen kernen zee es owsbessairn
There's a button missing	Hier fehlt ein Knopf	Heer faylt īn knopf
Will you sew on another one, please?	Würden Sie bitte einen anderen annähen?	Vuirden zee bitter īnen anderen an-nayen
I need them by this evening/tomorrow	Ich brauche sie bis heute abend/morgen	Ikh browkher zee bis hoyter ahbent/morgen
Call back at five o'clock	*Kommen Sie um fünf Uhr wieder	Kommen zee oom fuinf oor veedair
We can't do it before Tuesday	*Wir können es nicht vor Dienstag machen	Veer kernen es nikht fohr deenstag makhen
It will take three days	*Es dauert drei Tage	Es dowairt drī tahger
This isn't mine	Das gehört mir nicht	Das ge-hert meer nikht
I've lost my ticket	Ich habe meinen Zettel verloren	Ikh hahber mīnen tsettel fairlohren

HOUSEHOLD LAUNDRY

bath towel	das Badehandtuch	bahder-hant-tookh
blanket	die Wolldecke	volldecker
napkin	die Serviette	zairvyetter
pillow case	der Kissenbezug	kissenbetsoog
sheet	das Bettlaken	betlahken
tablecloth	das Tischtuch	tishtookh

NEWSPAPERS, BOOKS AND WRITING MATERIALS

Do you sell English/
American
newspapers/
magazines?

Verkaufen Sie
englische/
amerikanische
Zeitungen/
Zeitschriften?

Fairkowfen zee
englisher/
amaireekahnisher
tsītoongen/tsītshriften

Can you get ...
magazine for me?

Können Sie die
Zeitschrift ... für
mich besorgen?

Kernen zee dee tsītshrift
... fuir mikh bezorgen

Where can I get the
...?

Wo kann ich ...
bekommen?

Voh kan ikh ...
bekommen

I want a map of the
city/road map of ...

Ich möchte einen
Stadtplan/
Strassenplan von
...

Ikh merkhter īnen
shtatplahn/
shtrahssenplahn fon

I want an
entertainment/
amusements guide

Ich möchte ein
Veranstaltungs-
programm

Ikh merkhter īn
fairanshtaltoongs-
prohgram

Do you have any
English books?

Haben Sie englische
Bücher?

Hahben zee englisher
buikher

Have you any books by
...?

Haben Sie
irgendwelche
Bücher von ...?

Hahben zee
eergentvelkher buikher
fon

I want some picture
postcards/plain
postcards

Ich möchte einige
Ansichtskarten/
Postkarten

Ikh merkhter īniger
anzikhtskarten/
postkarten

Do you sell souvenirs/toys?	**Verkaufen Sie Reiseandenken/ Spielwaren?**	Fairkowfen zee rīzerandenken/ shpeelvahren
ballpoint	**der Kugelschreiber**	koogelshrīber
calculator	**der Rechner**	rekhnair
card	**die Karte**	karter
dictionary	**das Wörterbuch**	vertairbookh
drawing paper	**das Zeichenpapier**	tsīkhenpapeer
drawing pin	**die Reisszwecke**	rīstsveker
elastic band	**das Gummiband**	goomibant
envelope	**der Umschlag/das Kuvert**	oomshlag/kouvair
felt-tip pen	**der Filzstift**	filts-shtift
glue/paste	**der Leim/Klebstoff**	līm/klaybshtof
guide book	**der Führer**	fuirer
ink	**die Tinte**	tinter
notebook	**das Notizbuch**	nohteets-bookh
paperclip	**die Büroklammer**	buiroh-klammair
pen	**der Füllfederhalter**	fuillfaydairhaltair
pen cartridge	**die Patrone**	pahtrohner
pencil (coloured)	**der Bleistift (der Farbstift)**	blīshtift (farbshtift)
pencil sharpener	**der Anspitzer**	anshpitsair
postcard	**die Postkarte**	postkarter
rubber	**der Radiergummi**	rahdeergoommee
sellotape	**der Tesafilm**	tayzahfilm

| string | das Band | bant |
| (writing) paper | das (Schreib)papier | (shrīb)papeer |

OPTICIAN

I have broken my glasses; can you repair them?	Meine Brille ist kaputt; können Sie sie reparieren?	Mīner briller ist kahpoot kernen zee zee raypahreeren
Can you give me a new pair of glasses to the same prescription?	Können Sie mir eine neue Brille nach dem gleichen Rezept geben?	Kernen zee meer īner noyer briller nahkh daym glīkhen raytsept gayben
I have difficulty with reading	Ich habe Schwierigkeiten beim Lesen	Ikh hahber shveerikh-kīten bīm layzen
I have difficulty with long distance vision	Ich kann schlecht auf grössere Entfernung sehen	Ikh kan shlekht owf grersairer entfairnoong zayen
Please test my eyes	Bitte untersuchen Sie meine Augen	Bitter oontairzookhen zee mīner owgen
I have lost one of my contact lenses	Ich habe eine meiner Kontaktlinsen verloren	Ikh hahber īner mīnair kontaktlinzen fairlohren
I should like to have contact lenses	Ich hätte gern Kontaktlinsen	Ikh het-ter gern kontaktlinzen
I am short-sighted/long-sighted	Ich bin kurzsichtig/weitsichtig	Ikh bin koortszikhtikh/vītzikhtikh

PHOTOGRAPHY

want to buy a camera	Ich möchte eine Kamera kaufen	Ikh merkhter īner kamerah kowfen
Iave you a film/ cartridge for this camera, please?	Haben Sie einen Film/eine Filmpatrone für diesen (Foto)apparat?	Hahben zee īnen film/ īner filmpatrohner fuir deezen (fohtoh)aparaht
A 100/400/1000 ASA film, please	Einen 100/400/1000 ASA Film bitte	Īnen hoondairt/ feerhoondairt/towzent ah-es-ah film bitter
'ilm for slides/prints	Einen Film für Dias/Abzüge	Īnen film fuir deeahs/ aptsuiger
want a (fast) colour film/black-and-white film	Ich möchte einen (schnellen) Farbfilm/ schwarz-weiss Film	Ikh merkhter īnen (shnellen) farbfilm/ shvarts-vīs film
Vhat is the fastest film you have?	Welches ist der schnellste Film, den Sie haben?	Velkhes ist dair shnellster film dayn zee hahben
Vould you fit the film in the camera for me, please?	Würden Sie bitte den Film für mich in den Apparat einlegen	Vuirden zee bitter dayn film fuir mikh in dayn aparaht īn-laygen
)o you have flash bulbs?	Haben Sie Blitz-lichter?	Hahben zee blitslikhter
)oes the price include processing?	Schliesst dieser Preis das Entwickeln ein?	Shleest deezair prīs das entvickeln īn

I'd like this film developed and printed	Würden Sie diesen Film bitte entwickeln und abziehen?	Vuirden zee deezen film bitter entvickeln oont aptsee-en
Can I have … prints/ enlargements of this negative?	Können Sie mir … Abzüge/ Vergrösserungen von diesem Negativ machen?	Kernen zee meer … aptsuiger/ fairgrersairoongen fon deezem naygahteef makhen
When will it be ready?	Wann ist es fertig?	Van ist es fairtikh
Will it be done tomorrow?	Ist es morgen fertig?	Ist es morgen fairtikh
My camera's not working; can you look at it?	Meine Kamera funktioniert nicht; können Sie sie überprüfen?	Mīner kamerah foonktsyoneert nikht kernen zee zee uiberpruifen
The film is jammed	Der Film hat sich festgeklemmt	Dair film hat zikh festgeklemt
I need a (haze) filter/ lens cap	Ich brauche einen (Dunst) Filter/ Objektivdeckel	Ikh browkher īnen (doonst)filtair/ obyekteef-dekel
There is something wrong with the flash	Mit diesem Blitzlicht stimmt etwas nicht	Mit deezem blitslikht shtimt etvas nikht
battery	die Batterie	battairee
cine film	der Schmalfilm	shmahlfilm
filter	der Filter	filtair
lens	die Linse	linzer
lens cap	die Linsenkappe	linzenkapper
light meter	der Lichtmesser	likhtmessair
shutter	der Verschluss	fairshloos

RECORDS AND CASSETTES

Do you have any records/cassettes of local music?	**Haben Sie Platten/ Kassetten mit Musik aus dieser Gegend?**	Hahben zee **platten**/ kassetten mit moo-**zeek** ows **deezair gaygent**
Are there any new records by ...?	**Gibt es neue Platten von ...?**	Geept es **noyer platten** fon
Do you sell compact discs/video cassettes?	**Verkaufen Sie CDs/ Videokassetten?**	Fairkowfen zee tsay-days/**veedayoh**-kassetten

TOBACCONIST

Do you stock English/ American cigarettes?	**Haben Sie englische/ amerikanische Zigaretten?**	Hahben zee **englisher**/ amaireekahnisher tseegahretten
What cigarettes/cigars have you?	**Welche Zigaretten/ Zigarren haben Sie?**	Velkher tseegahretten/ tseegarren **hahben** zee
I want some filter tip cigarettes cigarettes without filter menthol cigarettes	**Ich möchte Filterzigaretten Zigaretten ohne Filter Zigaretten mit Menthol**	Ikh **merkhter** filtairtseegahretten tseegahretten **ohner** filter tseegahretten mit mentohl
A box of matches	**Eine Schachtel Streichhölzer**	Iner shakhtel **shtrikh**-herltser

Do you have cigarette paper/pipe cleaners?	**Haben Sie Zigarettenpapier/ Pfeifenreiniger?**	Hahben zee tseegahretten-papeer/ pfifen-rīneegair
I want to buy a lighter	**Ich möchte ein Feuerzeug kaufen**	Ikh merkhter īn foyairtsoyg kowfen
Do you sell lighter fuel/flints?	**Verkaufen Sie Feuerzeug-benzin/Flintsteine?**	Fairkowfen zee foyairtsoyg-bentseen/ flintshtīner
I want a gas refill	**Ich möchte eine neue Gasfüllung**	Ikh merkhter īner noyer gasfuilloong

REPAIRS

This is broken; could you mend it?	**Dies ist kaputt; können Sie es reparieren?**	Dees ist kapoot; kernen zee es raypahreeren
Could you do it while I wait?	**Können Sie es machen, während ich warte?**	Kernen zee es makhen vayrent ikh vahrter
When should I come back for it?	**Wann kann ich es abholen?**	Van kan ikh es aphohlen
I want these shoes soled (with leather)	**Ich möchte an diesen Schuhen (Leder)sohlen haben**	Ikh merkhter an deezen shoo-en (laydair)zohlen hahben
I want them heeled (with rubber)	**Ich möchte (Gummi)absätze haben**	Ikh merkhter (goommi)apsetser hahben

I have broken the heel; can you put on a new one?	Der Absatz ist gebrochen; können Sie einen neuen anmachen?	Dair apzats ist gebrokhen; kernen zee īnen noyen anmakhen
My watch is broken	Meine Uhr ist kaputt	Mīner oor ist kapoot
I have broken the glass/strap/spring	Das Glas/der Riemen/die Feder ist kaputt	Das glahs/dair reemen/ dee faydair ist kapoot
I have broken my glasses/the frame/ the arm	Meine Brille/der Rahmen/der Bügel ist kaputt	Mīner briller/dair rahmen/dair buigel ist kapoot
How much would a new one cost?	Wieviel kostet ein neuer/eine neue/ ein neues?	Veefeel kostet īn noyair/ īner noyair/īn noyes
The stone/charm/ screw has come loose	Der Stein/der Anhänger/die Schraube ist lose	Dair shtīn/dair anhengair/dee shrowber ist lohzer
The fastener/clip/ chain is broken	Der Verschluss/die Spange/die Kette ist kaputt	Dair fairshloos/dee shpanger/dee ketter ist kapoot
It can't be repaired	*Es kann nicht repariert werden	Es kan nikht raypahreert vairden

POST OFFICE

Where's the main post office?	**Wo ist die Hauptpost?**	Voh ist dee **howpt**-post
Where's the nearest post office?	**Wo ist die nächste Post?**	Voh ist dee **naikh**ster post
What time does the post office open/close?	**Wann macht die Post auf/zu?**	Van makht dee post owf/tsoo
Where's the post box?	**Wo ist der Briefkasten?**	Voh ist dair **breef**kasten
Which counter do I go to for stamps/money orders?	**An welchem Schalter bekomme ich Briefmarken/Postanweisungen?**	An velkhem **shal**tair bekommer ikh **breef**marken/**post**anvīzoongen
Where can I send a telegram?	**Wo kann ich ein Telegram aufgeben?**	Voh kan ikh īn tayle**gram** owfgayben

LETTERS AND TELEGRAMS

How much is a postcard to England?	Wie teuer ist eine Postkarte nach England?	Vee toyer ist iner postkarter nahkh englant
What's the airmail rate for letters to the USA?	Wie teuer ist Luftpost in die USA?	Vee toyer ist looftpost in dee oo-es-ah
How much is it to send a letter surface mail to the USA?	Wie teuer ist ein Brief per Schiffpost in die USA?	Vee toyer ist in breef pair shifpost in dee oo-es-ah
It's inland	Es ist fürs Inland	Es ist fuirs inlant
Give me three ... pfennig stamps, please	Geben Sie mir bitte drei Briefmarken zu ... Pfennig	Gayben zee meer bitter dri breefmarken tsoo ... pfennikh
I want to send this letter express	Ich möchte diesen Brief per Eilpost senden	Ikh merkhter deezen breef pair ilpost zenden
I want to register this letter	Ich möchte diesen Brief einschreiben	Ikh merkhter deezen breef inshriben
I want to send a parcel	Ich möchte ein Paket schicken	Ikh merkhter in pakayt shicken
Can I send a telex?	Kann ich ein Telex schicken?	Kan ikh in tayleks shicken
Where is the poste restante section?	Wo ist der Schalter 'Postlagernde Sendungen?'	Voh ist dair shaltair postlahgairnder zendoongen

Are there any letters for me?	**Sind Briefe für mich da?**	Zint breefer fuir mikh da?
What is your name?	***Wie ist Ihr Name?**	Vee ist eer **nahmer**
Have you any means of identification?	***Können Sie sich identifizieren (ausweisen)?**	Kernen zee zikh eedenteefeetseeren (owsvīzen)
I want to send a (reply paid) telegram	**Ich möchte ein Telegramm (mit bezahlter Antwort) senden**	Ikh **merkh**ter īn taylegram (mit betsahltair antvort) zenden
How much does it cost per word?	**Wieviel kostet es pro Wort?**	Veefeel kostet es pro vort
Write the message here and your own name and address	***Schreiben Sie den Text hier und Ihren eigenen Namen und Adresse**	Shrīben zee dayn tekst heer oont eeren īgenen nahmen oont addresser

TELEPHONING

Where's the nearest phone box?	**Wo ist die nächste Telefonzelle?**	Voh ist dee **naikh**ster tayle**fohn**-tseller
I want to make a phone call	**Ich möchte telefonieren**	Ikh **merkh**ter taylefohneeren
May I use your phone?	**Kann ich Ihr Telefon benutzen?**	Kan ikh eer tayle**fohn** benootsen
Do you have a telephone directory for ...?	**Haben Sie ein Telefonbuch für ...?**	Hahben zee īn tayle**fohn**bookh fuir

Please get me ...	Bitte verbinden Sie mich mit ...	Bitter fairbinden zee mikh mit
I want to telephone to England	Ich möchte nach England telefonieren	Ikh merkhter nahkh englant taylefohneeren
What do I dial to get the international operator?	Wie bekomme ich die internationale Vermittlung?	Vee bekommer ikh dee intair-natseeyonahler fairmittloong
What is the code for ...?	Wie ist die Vorwahlnummer für ...?	Vee ist dee forhvahl-noomair fuir
I want to place a personal (person-to-person) call	Ich möchte ein V-Gespräch führen	Ikh merkhter īn fow-geshpraykh fuiren
Could you give me the cost (time and charges) afterwards?	Könnten Sie mir hinterher die Gebühren angeben?	Kernten zee meer hintairhayr dee gebuihren angayben
I want to reverse the charges (call collect)	Ein R-Gespräch bitte	Īn air-geshpraykh bitter
I was cut off, can you reconnect me?	Ich wurde unterbrochen, können Sie mich wieder verbinden?	Ikh voorder oontairbrokhen kernen zee mikh veedair fairbinden
The number is out of order	*Die Nummer ist ausser Betrieb	Dee noomair ist owsair betreep
I want extension ...	Apparat ... bitte	Apparaht ... bitter
May I speak to ...?	Kann ich bitte ... sprechen?	Kan ikh bitter ... shprekhen
Who's speaking?	*Wer spricht da?	Vair shprikht dah

Hold the line, please	*Bleiben Sie bitte am Apparat	Blīben zee bitter am apparaht
Put the receiver down	*Legen Sie den Hörer auf	Laygen zee dayn herer owf
He's not here	*Er ist nicht hier	Air ist nikht heer
When will he be back?	Wann kommt er zurück?	Van kommt air tsooruik
Will you take a message	Würden Sie bitte etwas ausrichten?	Vuirden zee bitter etvas owsrikhten
Tell him that ... phoned	Sagen Sie ihm bitte, dass ... angerufen hat	Zahgen zee eem bitter das ... angeroofen hat
I'll ring again later	Ich rufe später wieder an	Ikh roofer shpayter veedair an
Please ask him to phone me	Bitten Sie ihn, mich anzurufen	Bitten zee een mikh antsooroofen
What's your number?	*Wie ist Ihre Nummer?	Vee ist eerer noomair
My number is ...	Meine Nummer ist ...	Mīner noomair ist
I can't hear you	Ich kann Sie nicht verstehen	Ikh kan zee nikht fairshtay-en
The line is engaged	*Die Leitung ist besetzt	Dee lītoong ist bezetst
There's no reply	*Es meldet sich niemand	Es meldet zikh neemant
You have the wrong number	*Sie sind falsch verbunden	Zee zint falsh fairboonden

SIGHTSEEING

Where is the tourist office?	Wo ist das Fremdenverkehrsbüro?	Voh ist das fremdenfairkayrsbuiroh
What should we see here?	Was sollten wir uns hier ansehen?	Vas zollten veer oons heer anzayen
Is there a map/plan of the places to visit?	Haben Sie einen Stadtplan mit den Sehenswürdigkeiten?	Hahben zee īnen shtatplahn mit dayn zayenzvuirdikh-kīten
I want a good guide book	Ich möchte einen guten Führer	Ikh merkhter īnen gooten fuirer
Is there a good sightseeing tour?	Gibt es eine gute Stadtrundfahrt?	Geept es īner gooter shtatroontfahrt
Does the coach stop at ... hotel?	Hält der Bus beim ... Hotel?	Helt dair boos bīm ... hohtel
Is there an excursion to ...?	Gibt es eine Ausflugsfahrt nach ...?	Geept es īner owsfloogsfahrt nahkh
How long does the tour take?	Wie lange dauert die Tour?	Vee langer dowairt dee toor

Are there guided tours of the museum?	Gibt es Museumsführungen?	Geept es moozayoomsfuiroongen
Does the guide speak English?	Spricht der Führer englisch?	Shprikht dair fuirer english
We don't need a guide	Wir brauchen keinen Führer	Veer browkhen kīnen fuirer
I would prefer to go round alone; is that all right?	Ich würde lieber alleine rumgehen wenn es recht ist	Ikh vuirder leebair allīner roomgayen ven es rekht ist
How much does the tour cost?	Wieviel kostet die Tour?	Veefeel kostet dee toor
Are all admission fees included?	Sind alle Eintrittsgebühren mit einbegriffen	Zint aller īntritsgebuiren mit īnbegriffen
Does it include lunch?	Ist das inklusive Mittagessen?	Ist das inkloozeever meetahgessen

MUSEUMS AND ART GALLERIES

When does the museum open/close?	Wann öffnet/ schliesst das Museum?	Van erfnet/shleest das moozayoom
Is it open every day?	Ist es jeden Tag geöffnet?	Ist es yayden tahg ge-erfnet
The gallery is closed on Mondays	*Die Galerie ist montags geschlossen	Dee gallairee ist mohntahgs geshlossen
How much does it cost?	Wieviel kostet es?	Veefeel kostet es

Are there reductions for children? students? the elderly?	Gibt es Ermässigungen für Kinder? Studenten? ältere Leute?	Geept es airmayseegoongen fuir kindair shtoodenten eltairer loyter
Are admission fees lower on any special day?	Gibt es an bestimmten Tagen eine Eintrittsermässigung?	Geept es an beshtimmten tahgen īner īntrits-airmayseegoong
Admission free	*Eintritt frei	Īntrit frī
Have you got a ticket?	*Haben Sie eine (Eintritts)Karte?	Hahben zee īner īntritskarter
Where do I buy a ticket?	Wo kaufe ich eine (Eintritts)Karte?	Voh kowfer ikh īner īntritskarter
Please leave your bag in the cloakroom	*Die Tasche bitte bei der Garderobe abgeben	Dee tasher bitter bī dair gardairrohber apgayben
It's over there	*Dort drüben	Dort druiben
Where is the ... collection/exhibition?	Wo ist die ... Sammlung/ Ausstellung?	Voh ist dee ... zamloong/ows-shtelloong
Can I take photographs?	Kann ich fotografieren?	Kan ikh fohtohgrahfeeren
Can I use a tripod?	Kann ich ein Stativ benutzen?	Kan ikh īn shtahteef benootsen
Photographs are not allowed	*Fotografieren ist nicht erlaubt	Fohtohgrahfeeren ist nikht airlowpt
I want to buy a catalogue	Ich möchte einen Katalog kaufen	Ikh merkhter īnen katalohg kowfen

Will you make photocopies?	Werden Sie Fotokopien davon machen?	Vairden zee fohtoh-kohpeeyen dahfon makhen
Could you make me a transparency of this painting?	Können Sie mir ein Dia von diesem Gemälde machen?	Kernen zee meer īn dee-ah fon deezem gemelder makhen
How long will it take?	Wie lange wird es dauern?	Vee langer veert es dowairn

HISTORICAL SITES

We want to visit ... can we get there by car?	Wir möchten ... besichtigen; können wir mit dem Wagen dahin fahren?	Veer merkhten ... bezikhteegen; kernen veer mit dem vahgen dah-hin fahren
Is it far to walk?	Ist es weit zu gehen?	Ist es vīt tsoo gayen
Is it an easy walk?	Ist es gut zu gehen?	Ist es goot tsoo gayen
Is there access for wheelchairs?	Ist es mit einem Rollstuhl zugänglich?	Ist es mit īnem rollshtool tsoogenglikh
Is it far	Ist es weit	Ist es vīt
to the aqueduct?	zum Aquädukt?	tsoom ahk-vaydookt
to the castle?	zum Schloss?	tsoom shloss
to the fort?	zum Fort?	tsoom fort
to the fortifications?	zu den Festungsanlagen?	tsoo dayn festoongzanlahgen
to the fountain?	zum Brunnen?	tsoom broonnen
to the gate?	zum Tor?	tsoom tohr
to the walls?	zur Mauer?	tsoor mowair

When was it built?	**Wann wurde es gebaut?**	Van voorder es gebowt
Who built it?	**Wer hat es gebaut?**	Vair hat es gebowt
Where is the old part of the city?	**Wo ist die Altstadt?**	Voh ist dee altshtat
What is the building?	**Was für ein Gebäude ist das?**	Vas fuir īn geboyder ist das
Where is ... house? ... church? ... cemetery?	**Wo ist** **das ... Haus?** **die ... Kirche?** **der ... Friedhof**	Voh ist das ... hows dee ... keerkher dair ... freedhohf

GARDENS, PARKS AND ZOOS

Where is the botanical garden/the zoo?	**Wo ist der botanische Garten/der Zoo?**	Voh ist dair bohtahneesher garten/ dair tsoh
How do I get to the park?	**Wie komme ich zum Park?**	Vee kommer ikh tsoom park
Can we walk there?	**Können wir dahin zu Fuss gehen?**	Kernen veer dah-hin tsoo foos gayen
Can we drive through the park?	**Können wir durch den Park fahren?**	Kernen veer doorkh dayn park fahren
Are the gardens open to the public?	**Ist die Gartenanlage der Öffentlichkeit zugänglich?**	Ist dee garten-anlahger dair erfentlikh-kīt tsoogenglikh
What time do the gardens close?	**Wann werden die Gartenanlagen geschlossen?**	Van vairden dee garten-anlahgen geshlossen

Is there a plan of the gardens?	Gibt es einen Plan der Gartenanlagen?	Geept es īnen plahn dair garten-anlahgen
Who designed the gardens?	Wer hat den Garten angelegt?	Vair hat dayn garten angelaygt
Where is the tropical plant house/the lake?	Wo ist das tropische Gewächshaus/der See?	Voh ist das trohpeesher geveks-hows/dair zay

EXPLORING

I'd like to walk round the old town	Ich möchte die Altstadt besichtigen	Ikh merkhter dee altshtat bezikhteegen
Is there a street plan showing the buildings?	Gibt es einen Stadtplan, der die sehenswerten Gebäude zeigt?	Geept es īnen shtatplahn dair dee zayenzvairten geboyder tsīgt
We want to visit the cathedral	Wir möchten den Dom besichtigen	Veer merkhten dayn dohm bezikhteegen
fortress	die Festung	dee festoong
library	die Bibliothek	dee beebleeyohtayk
monastery	das Kloster	das klohstair
palace	den Palast	dayn pahlast
ruins	die Ruine	dee roo-eener
May we walk around the walls?	Können wir um die Mauer herumgehen?	Kernen veer oom dee mowair hairoomgayen
go up the tower?	auf den Turm steigen?	owf dayn toorm shtīgen

| Where is the antiques market/the flea market? | Wo ist der Antiquitätenmarkt/ der Flohmarkt? | Voh ist dair anteekveetayten-markt/dair flohmarkt |

GOING TO CHURCH

Is there a Catholic church?	Gibt es hier eine katholische Kirche?	Geept es heer īner kahtohleesher keerkher
Protestant church?	protestantische Kirche?	prohtestanteesher keerkher
mosque?	Moschee?	mohshay
synagogue?	Synagoge?	zuinahgohger
What time is mass/the service?	Wann wird die Messe/der Gottesdienst gehalten?	Van weert dee messer/ dair gottesdeenst gehalten
I'd like to look round the church	Ich möchte die Kirche besichtigen	Ikh merkhter dee keerkher bezikhteegen
When was the church built?	Wann wurde die Kirche erbaut?	Van voorder dee keerkher airbowt
Should women cover their heads?	Müssen Frauen sich den Kopf bedecken?	Muissen frowen zikh dayn kopf bedeken

ENTERTAINMENT

Is there an entertainment guide?	Gibt es ein Veranstaltungs-programm?	Geept es īn fairanshtaltoongs-prohgram
What's on at the theatre/cinema?	Was wird im Theater/im Kino gespielt?	Vas veert im tayahtair/im keenoh geshpeelt
Is there a concert on?	Gibt es ein Konzert?	Geept es īn kontsairt
Can you recommend a good ballet? a good film? a good musical?	Können Sie ein gutes Ballett einen guten Film ein gutes Musical empfehlen?	Kernen zee īn gootes bahlet īnen gooten film īn gootes myoozikal empfaylen
Who is directing?	Wer führt Regie?	Vair fuirt rayshee
Who is conducting?	Wer dirigiert?	Vair deereegeert
Who is singing?	Wer singt?	Vair zingt

I want two seats for tonight/for the matinée tomorrow	Ich möchte zwei Plätze für heute abend/für die Matineevorstellung morgen	Ikh merkhter tsvī pletser fuir hoyter ahbent/fuir dee matinay-fohrshtelloong morgen
I want to book seats for Thursday	Ich möchte Plätze für Donnerstag bestellen	Ikh merkhter pletser fuir donnairstahg beshtellen
Is the matinée sold out?	Ist die Matineevorstellung ausverkauft?	Ist dee mateenay-fohrshtelloong owsfairkowft
I'd like seats in the stalls in the circle in the gallery	Ich möchte Plätze im Parkett im Rang im obersten Rang/Balkon	Ikh merkhter pletser im parket im rang im ohbairsten rang/balkohn
The cheapest seats please	Die billigsten Plätze bitte	Dee billeegsten pletser bitter
That performance is sold out	*Die Vorstellung ist ausverkauft	Dee fohrshtelloong ist owsfairkowft
Are they good seats?	Sind es gute Plätze?	Zint es gooter pletser
Where are these seats?	Wo sind diese Plätze?	Voh zint deezer pletser
When does the curtain go up?	Wann geht der Vorhang auf?	Van gayt dair fohrhang owf
What time does the performance end?	Wann ist die Vorstellung zu Ende?	Van ist dee fohrshtelloong tsoo ender
Where is the cloakroom?	Wo ist die Garderobe?	Voh ist dee garderohber

This is your seat	*Hier ist Ihr Platz	Heer ist eer plats
A programme, please	Ein Programm bitte	In program bitter
What's the best nightclub?	Welches ist der beste Nachtklub?	Velkhes ist dair bester nakhtkloob
What time is the floorshow?	Wann beginnt das Kabarett?	Van beginnt das kabahrett
Is there a jazz club here?	Gibt es hier einen Jazz-Club?	Geept es heer inen dshass-kloop
Can you recommend a good show?	Können Sie eine gute Veranstaltung empfehlen?	Kernen zee iner gooter fairanshtaltoong empfaylen
Where can we go dancing?	Wo können wir tanzen?	Voh kernen veer tantsen
Where is the best disco?	Wo ist die beste Disko?	Voh ist dee bester diskoh
Would you like to dance?	Möchten Sie tanzen?	Merkhten zee tantsen

SPORTS & GAMES

Where is the nearest tennis court/golf course?	Wo ist der nächste Tennisplatz/ Golfplatz?	Voh ist dair naikhster tennis-plats/golfplats
What is the charge per game? hour? day?	Was kostet es pro Spiel? Stunde? Tag?	Vas kostet es pro shpeel shtoonder tahg
Is it a club?	Ist es ein Klub?	Ist es īn kloop
Do I need temporary membership?	Muss ich vorübergehend Mitglied werden?	Moos ikh fohruibair-gayent mitgleed vairden
Where can we go swimming/fishing?	Wo können wir schwimmen/ angeln?	Voh kernen veer shvimmen/angeln
Can I hire a racket? clubs? fishing tackle?	Kann ich einen Schläger Golfschläger Angelzeug mieten?	Kan ikh īnen shlaygair golfshlaygair angeltsoykh meeten

Do I need a permit?	**Brauche ich eine Genehmigung?**	Browkher ikh īner genaymeegoong
Where do I get a permit?	**Wo bekomme ich eine Genehmigung?**	Voh bekommer ikh īner genaymeegoong
Can we swim in the river?	**Können wir im Fluss baden?**	Kernen veer im floos bahden
Is there an open air/indoor swimming pool?	**Gibt es hier ein Freibad/Hallenbad?**	Geept es heer īn frībat/hallenbat
Is it heated?	**Ist es erwärmt?**	Ist es airvermt
Is there a skating rink (ice)/roller)?	**Gibt es hier eine Eisbahn/Rollschuhbahn?**	Geept es heer īner īsbahn/rollshoobahn
Can I hire skates/skiing equipment?	**Kann ich Schlittschuhe/eine Skiausrüstung mieten?**	Kan ikh shlitshooer/īner shee-owsruistoong meeten
Can I take lessons here?	**Geben Sie hier Unterricht?**	Gayben zee heer oontair-rikht
I've never skied before	**Ich bin noch nie Ski gelaufen**	Ikh bin nokh nee shee gelowfen
Are there ski runs for beginners/average skiers?	**Gibt es Pisten für Anfänger/mittelmässige Skiläufer?**	Geept es pisten fuir anfengair/mittelmayseeger sheeloyfair
I'd like to go cross-country skiing	**Ich möchte Langstrecken laufen**	Ikh merkhter langshtreken lowfen

Are there ski lifts?	Gibt es hier Skilifts?	Geept es heer sheelifts
We want to go to a football match/the tennis tournament	Wir möchten uns ein Fussballspiel/das Tennisturnier ansehen	Veer merkhten oons īn foosballshpeel/das tennistoorneer anzayen
Can you get us tickets?	Können Sie uns Karten besorgen?	Kernen zee oons karten bezorgen
Are there seats in the grandstand?	Gibt es noch Plätze auf der Haupttribüne?	Geept es nokh pletser owf dair howpt-treebuiner
How much are the cheapest seats?	Wieviel kosten die billigsten Plätze?	Veefeel kosten dee billeegsten pletser
Who is playing?	Wer spielt?	Vair shpeelt
When does it start?	Wann fängt es an?	Van fengt es an
Who is winning?	Wer gewinnt?	Vair gevinnt
What is the score?	Wie steht es?	Vee shtayt es
I'd like to ride	Ich möchte gerne reiten	Ikh merkhter gairner rīten
Is there a riding stable nearby?	Gibt es hier einen Reitstall in der Nähe?	Geebt es heer īnen rīt-shtall in dair nayer
Do you give lessons?	Geben Sie Unterricht?	Gayben zee oontair-rikht
I am an inexperienced rider	Ich kann noch nicht gut reiten	Ikh kan nokh nikht goot rīten
I am a good rider	Ich kann gut reiten	Ikh kan goot rīten
Where is the race course?	Wo ist die Pferderennbahn?	Voh ist dee pfairder-rennbahn

Which is the favourite?	**Wer ist Favorit?**	Vair ist fahvohreet
Who is the jockey?	**Wer ist der Jockai?**	Vair ist dair yokee
... (*amount*) to win on ...	**... auf den Sieg von ...**	... owf dayn zeeg fon ...
... (*amount*) for a place ...	**... für eine Platzwette**	... fuir īner platsvetter
What are the odds?	**Wie stehen die Chancen?**	Vee shtayen dee dshansen
I'd like to try waterskiing	**Ich möchte versuchen, Wasserski zu laufen**	Ikh merkhter fairzookhen vassairshee tsoo lowfen
I haven't waterskied before	**Ich bin noch nie Wasserski gelaufen**	Ikh bin nokh nee vassairshee gelowfen
Can I borrow a wetsuit?	**Kann ich einen Taucheranzug leihen?**	Kan ikh īnen towkhair-anzoog lī-en
Should I wear a life jacket?	**Muss ich eine Schwimmweste tragen?**	Moos ikh īner shvimvester trahgen
Can I hire a rowing boat? a motor boat? wind surfer?	**Kann ich ein Ruderboot ein Motorboot ein Windsurfboard mieten?**	Kan ikh īn roodairboht īn mohtorboht īn vintserfbort meeten
Is there a map of the river?	**Gibt es eine Karte von diesem Fluss?**	Geept es īner karter fon deezem floos
Are there many locks to pass?	**Muss man durch viele Schleusen?**	Moos man doorkh feeler shloyzen

Can we get fuel here?	**Können wir hier tanken?**	Kernen veer heer **tanken**
Do you play cards?	**Spielen Sie Karten?**	**Shpeelen** zee **karten**
Would you like a game of chess?	**Möchten Sie Schach spielen?**	**Merkhten** zee shakh **shpeelen**

ON THE BEACH[1]

Which is the best beach?	**Welches ist der beste Strand?**	Velkhes ist dair bester shtrant
Is there a quiet beach near here?	**Gibt es einen ruhigen Strand in der Nähe?**	Geept es īnen rooigen shtrant in dair nayer
Is it far to walk?	**Ist es weit zu gehen?**	Ist es vīt tsoo gayen
Is there a bus to the beach?	**Fährt ein Bus zum Strand?**	Fairt īn boos tsoom shtrant
Is the beach sand/pebbles/rocks?	**Ist es ein Sand-/Kies-/Felsstrand?**	Ist es īn zant/kees/fels-shtrant
Is it safe for swimming?	**Kann man hier ohne Gefahr baden?**	Kan man heer ohner gefahr bahden
Is there a lifeguard?	**Gibt es hier einen Rettungsdienst?**	Geept es heer īnen rettoongs-deenst

1. See also SPORTS AND GAMES, p. 157.

Is it safe for small children?	**Können kleine Kinder hier ohne Gefahr baden?**	Kernen klīner kindair heer ohner gefahr bahden
Bathing prohibited/at own risk	***Baden verboten/auf eigene Gefahr**	Bahden fairbohten/owf īgener gefahr
Does it get very rough?	**Wird das Wasser sehr bewegt?**	Veert das vassair zayr bevaygt
It's dangerous	***Es ist gefährlich**	Es ist gefairlikh
What time is high/low tide?	**Wann ist Flut/Ebbe?**	Van ist floot/ebber
Is the tide rising/ falling?	**Steigt/fällt das Wasser?**	Shtīgt/fellt das vassair
There's a strong current here	***Die Strömung ist hier sehr stark**	Dee shtrermoong ist heer zayr shtark
It's very deep here	***Es ist hier sehr tief**	Es ist heer zayr teef
Are you a strong swimmer?	***Sind Sie ein tüchtiger Schwimmer?**	Zint zee īn tuikhtigair shvimmair
How's the water? Cold?	**Wie ist das Wasser? Kalt?**	Vee ist das vassair? Kalt?
It's warm	**Es ist warm**	Es ist varm
Can one swim in the lake/river?	**Kann man im See/ im Fluss baden?**	Kan man im zay/im floos bahden
Is there an indoor/ outdoor swimming pool?	**Gibt es ein Hallenbad/ein Freibad?**	Geept es īn hallenbat/īn frībat
Is it salt or fresh water?	**Ist es Salz- oder Süsswasser?**	Ist es zalts- ohdair zuissvassair
Are there showers?	**Gibt es Duschen?**	Geept es dooshen

I want to hire a cabin for the day/ morning/two hours	Ich möchte eine Kabine mieten für den Tag/für den Morgen/für zwei Stunden	Ikh merkhter īner kabeener meeten fuir dayn tahg/fuir dayn morgen/fuir tsvī shtoonden
I want to hire a deckchair/sunshade	Ich möchte einen Liegestuhl/ Sonnenschirm mieten	Ikh merkhter īnen leegershtool/ zonnenshirm meeten
Where's the harbour?	Wo ist der Hafen?	Voh ist dair hahfen
Can we go out in a fishing boat?	Können wir in einem Fischkutter hinausfahren?	Kernen veer in īnem fishkoottair hinowsfahren
Is there any underwater fishing?	Kann man unter Wasser fischen?	Kan man oontair vassair fishen
Can I hire a rowing/ motor/sailing boat?	Kann ich ein Ruderboot/ Motorboot/ Segelboot mieten?	Kan ikh īn roodairboht/ motohrboht/zaygelboht meeten
What does it cost by the hour?	Wieviel kostet ein Boot pro Stunde?	Veefeel kostet īn boht proh shtoonder
Where can I buy a snorkel? flippers? a bucket and spade?	Wo kann ich einen Schnorchel Schwimmflossen einen Eimer und eine Schaufel kaufen?	Voh kan ikh īnen shnorkhel shvimflossen īnen īmair oont īner showfel kowfen

IN THE COUNTRY[1]

Is there a scenic route to ...?	Gibt es eine 'grüne Strasse' nach ...?	Geept es īner gruiner shtrahsser nahkh
Can you give me a lift to ...?	Können Sie mich bis ... mitnehmen?	Kernen zee mikh bis ... mitnaymen
Is there a footpath to ...?	Führt ein Wanderweg nach ...?	Fuirt īn vandairvayg nahkh
Is it possible to go across country?	Kann man querfeldein gehen?	Kan man kvayr-feltīn gayen
Is there a shortcut?	Gibt es einen kürzeren Weg?	Geept es īnen kuirtsairen vayg
Is this a public footpath?	Ist dies ein öffentlicher Fussweg?	Ist dees īn erfentlikhair foosvayg

1. See also DIRECTIONS p. 35.

Is there a bridge across the stream?	**Führt eine Brücke über den Fluss?**	Fuirt **ī**ner **bruiker** uiber dayn floos
Can we walk?	**Können wir zu Fuss gehen?**	**Kern**en veer tsoo foos gayen
How far is the next village?	**Wie weit ist es bis zum nächsten Dorf?**	Vee v**ī**t ist es bis tsoom **naihkh**sten dorf

THE WEATHER

Is it usually as hot as this?	**Ist es immer so warm wie jetzt?**	Ist es **immair** zoh varm vee yetst
It's going to be hot/cold today	***Es wird heute warm/kalt werden**	Es veert **hoy**ter varm/kalt **vair**den
The mist will clear later	***Der Nebel wird sich auflösen**	Dair **nay**bel veert zikh **owf**lerzen
Will it be fine tomorrow?	**Wird es morgen schön?**	Veert es **mor**gen shern
What is the weather forecast?	**Wie ist der Wetterbericht?**	Vee ist dair **vettairbayrikht**
What lovely/awful weather!	**Was für ein schönes/scheussliches Wetter!**	Vas fuir **ī**n **sher**nes/**shoys**likhes **vet**tair
Will it rain/snow?	**Werden wir Regen/Schnee bekommen?**	**Vair**den veer **ray**gen/shnay be**kommen**

TRAVELLING WITH CHILDREN

Can you put a child's bed/cot in our room?	**Können Sie ein Kinderbett in unser Zimmer stellen?**	Kernen zee īn kindairbet in oonzair tsimmair shtellen
Can you give us an adjoining room?	**Können Sie uns Zimmer nebeneinander geben?**	Kernen zee oons tsimmair nayben-īnandair gayben
Does the hotel have a babysitting service?	**Hat das Hotel einen Babysitting Service?**	Hat das hohtel īnen baybeesitting sairvees
Can you find me a babysitter?	**Können Sie mir einen Babysitter besorgen?**	Kernen zee meer īnen baybeesittair bezorgen
We shall be out for a couple of hours	**Wir gehen auf etwa zwei Stunden aus**	Veer gayen owf etvah tsvī shtoonden ows

We shall be back at ...	Wir kommen um ... zurück	Veer kommen oom ... tsooruik
Is there a children's menu?	Haben Sie eine Kinderkarte?	Hahben zee iner kindair-karter
Do you have half-portions for children?	Haben Sie halbe Portionen für Kinder?	Hahben zee halber portsyohnen fuir kindair
Have you got a high chair?	Haben Sie einen Kinderstuhl?	Hahben zee inen kindairshtool
May we bring the pushchair in?	Können wir den Kinderwagen reinbringen?	Kernen veer dayn kindairvahgen rinbringen
Can you warm this milk please?	Können Sie diese Milch bitte warm machen?	Kernen zee deezer milkh bitter varm makhen
Can we have some hot water please?	Können wir bitte etwas heisses Wasser haben?	Kernen veer bitter etvas hisses vassair hahben
Are there any organized activities for children?	Gibt es irgend welche Kinderveranstaltungen?	Geept es eergent velkher kindair-fairanshtaltoongen
Is there a paddling pool? a children's swimming pool? a playground? a games room?	Gibt es ein Planschbecken? ein Schwimmbad für Kinder? einen Kinderspielplatz? ein Spielzimmer?	Geept es in planshbecken in shvimmbat fuir kindair inen kindairshpeelplats in shpeeltsimmair

Is there	Gibt es	Geept es
an amusement park	einen Vergnügungspark	**īnen** fairgnuigoongspark
a zoo	einen Zoo	**īnen** tsoh
a toyshop nearby?	ein Spielwarengeschäft in der Nähe?	**īn shpeelvahrengeheft** in dair nayer
I'd like	Ich möchte	Ikh **merkhter**
a beach ball	einen Strandball	**īnen shtrantball**
a bucket and spade	einen Eimer und eine Schaufel	**īnen īmair** oont **īner** showfel
a doll	eine Puppe	**īner pooper**
some flippers	Schwimmflossen	shvimflossen
some goggles	eine Schutzbrille	**īner shootsbriller**
some playing cards	Spielkarten	shpeelkarten
some roller skates	Rollschuhe	rollshooer
a snorkel	einen Schnorchel	**īnen shnorkhel**
Where can I change my baby?	Wo kann ich meinem Baby die Windeln wechseln?	Voh kan ikh **mīnem** baybee dee vindeln vekseln
Where can I feed my baby?	Wo kann ich mein Baby stillen?	Voh kan ikh **mīn baybee** shtillen
Can you heat this bottle for me?	Können Sie diese Flasche für mich warm machen?	Kernen zee **deezer** flasher fuir mikh varm makhen
I want	Ich möchte	Ikh **merkhter**
some disposable nappies	Papierwindeln	pahpeervindeln
a feeding bottle	eine Babyflasche	**īner** baybee-flasher
some baby food	Babynahrung	baybeenahroong

My daughter suffers from travel sickness	**Meine Tochter leidet unter Reisekrankheit**	Mīner tokhtair līdet oontair rīzer-krankhīt
She has hurt herself	**Sie hat sich verletzt**	Zee hat zikh fairletst
My son is ill	**Mein Sohn ist krank**	Mīn zohn ist krank
He has lost his toy	**Er hat sein Spielzeug verloren**	Ayr hat zīn shpeeltsoykh fairlohren
I'm sorry if they have bothered you	**Es tut mir leid, wenn sie Sie gestört haben**	Es toot meer līt ven zee zee geshtert hahben

BUSINESS MATTERS[1]

I would like to make an appointment with ...	Ich möchte einen Termin vereinbaren mit ...	Ikh merkhter īnen tairmeen fairīnbahren mit
I have an appointment with ...	Ich habe eine Verabredung mit ...	Ikh hahber īner fairapraydoong mit
My name is ...	Mein Name ist ...	Mīn nahmer ist
Here is my card	Hier ist meine Karte	Heer ist mīner karter
This is our catalogue	Dies ist unser Katalog	Dees ist oonzair katalohg
I would like to see your products	Ich möchte Ihre Erzeugnisse sehen	Ikh merkhter eerer airtsoygnisser zayen
Could you send me some samples?	Könnten Sie mir einige Muster schicken?	Kernten zee meer īniger moostair shicken

See also TELEPHONING, p. 144.

Can you provide an interpreter/a secretary?	**Haben Sie einen Dolmetscher/eine Sekretärin?**	Hahben zee īnen dolmetshair/īner zekretayrin
Where can I make some photocopies?	**Wo kann ich einige Fotokopien machen?**	Voh kan ikh īniger fohtohkohpee-yen makhen
Call back tomorrow	***Rufen Sie morgen früh wieder an**	Roofen zee morgen frui veedair an
You can contact me under this number ...	**Sie können mich unter dieser Nummer erreichen ...**	Zee kernen mikh oontair deezair noomair air-rīkhen
My telephone number is ...	**Meine Telefonnummer ist ...**	Mīner taylayfohn-noomair ist

AT THE DOCTOR'S

there a doctor's surgery near here?	Gibt es hier in der Nähe eine Arztpraxis?	Geept es heer in dair nayer īner artstpraxis
must see a doctor; can you recommend one?	Ich muss zum Arzt; können Sie mir einen empfehlen?	Ikh moos tsoom artst kernen zee meer īnen empfaylen
ease call a doctor	Bitte, rufen Sie einen Arzt	Bitter roofen zee īnen artst
hen can the doctor come?	Wann kann der Arzt kommen?	Van kan dair artst kommen
oes the doctor speak English?	Spricht der Arzt englisch?	Shprikht dair artst english
an I make an appointment for as soon as possible?	Kann ich mich für sobald wie möglich anmelden?	Kan ikh mikh fuir zohbalt vee merglikh anmelden

AILMENTS

I am ill	Ich bin krank	Ikh bin krank
I have high/low blood pressure	Ich habe hohen/ niedrigen Blutdruck	Ikh hahber hohen/ needreegen blootdrook
I am pregnant	Ich bin schwanger	Ikh bin shvangair
I am allergic to ...	Ich bin allergisch gegen ...	Ikh bin allairgeesh gaygen ...
I think it is infected	Ich glaube, es hat sich entzündet	Ikh glowber es hat zikh ent-tsuindet
I have a fever	Ich habe Fieber	Ikh hahber feebair
I've a pain in my right arm	Ich habe Schmerzen im rechten Arm	Ikh hahber shmairtsen im rekhten arm
My wrist hurts	Mein Handgelenk tut mir weh	Mīn hant-gelenk toot meer vay
I think I've sprained/ broken my ankle	Ich glaube, ich habe mir den Fuss verstaucht/den Knöchel gebrochen	Ikh glowber ikh hahber meer dayn foos fairshtowkht/dayn knerkhel gebrokhen
I fell down and hurt my back	Ich bin hingefallen und habe mir den Rücken verletzt	Ikh bin hingefallen oont hahber meer dayn ruiken fairletst
My foot is swollen	Mein Fuss ist geschwollen	Mīn foos ist geshvollen
I've burned/cut/ bruised myself	Ich habe mich verbrannt/ geschnitten/ gestossen	Ikh hahber mikh fairbrant/geshnitten/ geshtohssen

My stomach is upset	Ich habe Magenbeschwerden	Ikh hahber mahgen-beshvairden
My appetite's gone	Ich habe den Appetit verloren	Ikh hahber dayn appeteet fairlohren
I think I've got food poisoning	Ich glaube, ich habe eine Lebensmittel-vergiftung	Ikh glowber ikh hahber īner laybinsmittel-fair-giftoong
I can't eat/sleep	Ich kann nicht essen/schlafen	Ikh kan nikht essen/shlahfen
My nose keeps bleeding	Meine Nase blutet immer	Mīner nahzer blootet immair
I have difficulty in breathing	Ich habe Schwierigkeiten beim Atmen	Ikh hahber shveerikhkīten bīm ahtmen
I feel dizzy/sick	Mir ist schwindlig/schlecht	Meer ist shvindlikh/shlekht
I feel shivery	Mich fröstelt	Mikh frerstelt
I keep vomiting	Ich muss mich immer übergeben	Ikh moos mikh immair uibergayben
I think I've caught flu	Ich glaube, ich habe Grippe	Ikh glowber ikh hahber gripper
I've got a cold	Ich habe eine Erkältung	Ikh hahber īner airkeltoong
I've had it since yesterday/for a few hours	Ich habe es seit gestern/ein paar Stunden	Ikh hahber es zīt gestairn/īn pahr shtoonden
abscess	das Geschwür	geshvuir
ache	der Schmerz	shmairts

allergy	**die Allergie**	allairgee
asthma	**das Asthma**	astmah
back pain	**die Rückenschmerzen**	ruickenshmairtsen
blister	**die Blase**	blahzer
boil	**der Furunkel**	fooroonkel
bruise	**die Quetschung**	kvetshoong
burn	**die Brandwunde**	brantvoonder
cardiac condition	**der Herzfehler**	hairts-faylair
chill/cold	**die Erkältung**	airkeltoong
constipation	**die Verstopfung**	fairshtopfoong
cough	**der Husten**	hoosten
cramp	**der Krampf**	krampf
diabetic	**zuckerkrank**	tsoockerkrank
diarrhoea	**der Durchfall**	doorkhfal
earache	**die Ohrenschmerzen**	ohrenshmairtsen
fever	**das Fieber**	feebair
food poisoning	**die Lebensmittel-vergiftung**	laybensmittel-fairgiftoong
fracture	**der Bruch**	brookh
hay-fever	**der Heuschnupfen**	hoyshnoopfen
headache	**die Kopfschmerzen**	kopfshmairtsen
heart condition, (to have)	**herzleidend sein**	hairtslīdent zīn
high blood pressure	**der hohe Blutdruck**	hoher blootdrook
ill, sick	**krank**	krank

illness	die Krankheit	krankhīt
ill, sick	krank	krank
illness	die Krankheit	krankhīt
indigestion	die Verdauungsstörung	fairdowoongs-shter-roong
infection	die Ansteckung	ansteckoong
influenza	die Grippe	gripper
insect bite	der Insektenstich	inzektenshtikh
insomnia	die Schlaflosigkeit	shlahf-lohsikh-kīt
itch	das Jucken	yooken
nausea	die Übelkeit	uibel-kīt
nose bleed	das Nasenbluten	nahzenblooten
pain	der Schmerz	shmairts
rheumatism	der Rheumatismus	roymatizmoos
sore throat	die Halsschmerzen	hals-shmairtsen
sprain	die Verstauchung	fairshtowkhoong
sting	der Stich	shtikh
stomach ache	die Magenschmerzen	mahgen-shmairtsen
sunburn	der Sonnenbrand	zonnen-brant
sunstroke	der Sonnenstich	zonnen-shtikh
swelling	die Schwellung	shvelloong
tonsillitis	die Mandelentzündung	mandel-enttsuindoong
toothache	die Zahnschmerzen	tsahn-shmairtsen
ulcer	das Geschwür	geshvuir
wound	die Wunde	voonder

TREATMENT

You're hurting me	Sie tun mir weh	Zee toon meer vay
Must I stay in bed?	Muss ich im Bett bleiben?	Moos ikh im bett blīben
Will you call again?	Kommen Sie wieder?	Kommen zee veedair
How much do I owe you?	Wieviel schulde ich Ihnen?	Veefeel shoolder ikh eenen
When can I travel again?	Wann kann ich wieder reisen?	Van kan ikh veedair rīzen
I feel better now	Mir geht es jetzt wieder besser	Meer gayt es yetst veedair besser
Do you have a temperature?	*Haben Sie erhöhte Temperatur?	Hahben zee erherter tempairatoor
Where does it hurt?	*Wo tut es weh?	Voh toot es vay
Have you a pain here?	*Haben Sie hier Schmerzen?	Hahben zee heer shmairtsen
How long have you had the pain?	*Seit wann haben Sie die Schmerzen?	Zīt van hahben zee dee shmairtsen
Does that hurt?	*Tut das weh?	Toot das vay
A lot?	*Sehr?	Zayr
A little?	*Ein wenig?	Īn vaynikh
Open your mouth	*Machen Sie den Mund auf	Makhen zee dayn moont owf
Put out your tongue	*Stecken Sie die Zunge raus	Shteken zee dee tsoonger rows
Breathe in/out	*Atmen Sie ein/aus	Ahtmen zee īn/ows

Please lie down	*Legen Sie sich bitte hin	Laygen zee zikh bitter hin
I will need a specimen	*Ich brauche eine Urinprobe	Ikh browkher īner ooreen-prohber
What medicines have you been taking?	*Welche Medikamente haben Sie eingenommen?	Velkher maydikamenter hahben zee īn-genommen
I take this medicine; could you give me another prescription?	Ich nehme dieses Medikament ein; können Sie mir noch ein Rezept geben?	Ikh naymer deezes maydikament īn kernen zee meer nokh īn raytsept gayben
I will give you an antibiotic some medicine a painkiller	*Ich gebe Ihnen ein Antibiotikum Arznei (Medizin) ein schmerzstillendes Mittel	Ikh gayber eenen īn anteebeeohteekoom artsnī (maydietseen) īn shmairts-stillendes mittel
some pills a sedative some tablets	Pillen ein Beruhigungsmittel Tabletten	pillen īn bayrooyeegoongsmittel tabletten
Take this prescription to the chemist's	*Bringen Sie dieses Rezept in die Apotheke	Bringen zee deezes raytsept in dee apohtayker
Take this three times a day	*Nehmen Sie dies dreimal täglich ein	Naymen zee dees drīmahl tayglikh īn
I'll give you an injection	*Ich gebe Ihnen eine Spritze	Ikh gayber eenen īner shpritser
I'll put you on a diet	*Ich werde Sie auf Diät setzen	Ikh vairder zee owf dee-ayt zetsen

Come and see me again in two days' time	*Kommen Sie in zwei Tagen wieder	Kommen zee in tsvī tahgen veedair
You must be X-rayed	*Sie müssen geröntgt werden	Zee muissen gayrernkht vairden
You must go to the hospital	*Sie müssen ins Krankenhaus	Zee muissen ins krankenhows
You must stay in bed	*Sie müssen im Bett bleiben	Zee muissen im bett blīben
You should not travel until ...	*Sie sollten bis ... nicht reisen	Zee zollten bis ... nikht rīzen
Nothing to worry about	*Es besteht kein Grund zur Unruhe	Es beshtayt kīn groont tsoor oonroo-er
I'd like a receipt for the health insurance	Ich möchte eine Quittung für die Krankenversicherung	Ikh merkhter īner kvittoong fuir dee krankenfairzeekhairoong
ambulance	der Krankenwagen	kranken-vahgen
anaesthetic	das Betäubungsmittel	betoyboongs-mittel
aspirin	das Aspirin	aspeereen
bandage	der Verband	fairbant
chiropodist	der Fusspfleger	foos-pflaygair
hospital	das Krankenhaus	kranken-hows
injection	die Spritze	shpritser
laxative	das Abführmittel	apfuir-mittel
nurse	die (Kranken)schwester	(kranken)shvester
operation	die Operation	operats-yohn
optician	der Optiker	opteekair

osteopath	der Osteopath	ostayoh**paht**
pill	die Tablette	tabletter
(adhesive) plaster	das Pflaster	pflastair
prescription	das Rezept	raytsept
X-ray	die Röntgenaufnahme	rerntgen-owfnahmer

PARTS OF THE BODY

ankle	der Fussknöchel	foos-k-nerkhell
arm	der Arm	ahrm
back	der Rücken	ruiken
bladder	die Blase	blahzer
blood	das Blut	bloot
body	der Körper	kerpair
bone	der Knochen	k-nokhen
bowels	der Darm	darm
brain	das Gehirn	geheern
breast	die Brust	broost
cheek	die Wange	vanger
chest	die Brust	broost
chin	das Kinn	kin
collar-bone	das Schlüsselbein	shluisselbīn
ear	das Ohr	ohr
elbow	der Ellbogen	elbohgen
eye	das Auge	owger

eyelid	das Augenlid	owgenleed
face	das Gesicht	gezikht
finger	der Finger	finger
foot	der Fuss	foos
forehead	die Stirn	shteern
gums	das Zahnfleisch	tsahnflīsch
hand	die Hand	hant
head	der Kopf	kopf
heart	das Herz	hairts
heel	die Ferse	fairzer
hip	die Hüfte	huifter
jaw	der Kiefer	keefer
joint	das Gelenk	gelenk
kidney	die Niere	neerer
knee	das Knie	k-nee
knee-cap	die Kniescheibe	k-nee-shīber
leg	das Bein	bīn
lip	die Lippe	lipper
liver	die Leber	laybair
lung	die Lunge	loonger
mouth	der Mund	moont
muscle	der Muskel	mooskel
nail	der Nagel	nahgel
neck	der Hals	hals
nerve	der Nerv	nairf
nose	die Nase	nahzer

rib	die Rippe	ripper
shoulder	die Schulter	schooltair
skin	die Haut	howt
spine	das Rückgrat	ruikgraht
stomach	der Magen	mahgen
temple	die Schläfe	shlefer
thigh	der Schenkel	shenkel
throat	der Hals	hals
thumb	der Daumen	dowmen
toe	der Zeh	tsay
tongue	die Zunge	tsoonger
tonsils	die Mandeln	mandeln
tooth	der Zahn	tsahn
vein	die Ader	ahdair
wrist	das Handgelenk	hant-gelenk

AT THE DENTIST'S

I must see a dentist	**Ich muss zum Zahnarzt**	Ikh moos tsoom **tsahn-artst**
Can I make an appointment?	**Kann ich mich anmelden?**	Kan ikh mikh **anmelden**
As soon as possible, please	**Sobald wie möglich bitte**	Zohbalt vee **merglikh** bitter
I have toothache	**Ich habe Zahnschmerzen**	Ikh **hahber tsahn-shmairtsen**
This tooth hurts	**Dieser Zahn tut weh**	Deezair tsahn toot vay
I've lost a filling	**Ich habe eine Füllung (Plombe) verloren**	Ikh **hahber iner fuilloong (plomber) fairlohren**
Can you fill it?	**Können Sie ihn plombieren (füllen)?**	Kernen zee een plombeeren (fuillen)
Can you do it now?	**Können Sie es jetzt machen?**	Kernen zee es yetst makhen

I have a broken tooth/ an abscess	Ich habe einen kaputten Zahn/ einen Abszess	Ikh hahber īnen kapooten tsahn/īnen aptsess
I do not want the tooth taken out	Ziehen Sie den Zahn bitte nicht	Tseeyen zee dayn tsahn bitter nikht
Please give me an injection first	Bitte geben Sie mir zuerst eine Spritze (örtliche Betäubung)	Bitter gayben zee meer tsoo-airst īner shpritser (ertlikher betoyboong)
Please give me an anaesthetic	Bitte geben Sie mir eine Narkose	Bitter gayben zee meer īner nahrkohzer
My gums are swollen/ keep bleeding	Mein Zahnfleisch ist geschwollen/blutet immer	Mīn tsahnflīsh ist geshvollen/blootet immair
I have broken/chipped my dentures	Meine Zahnprotese ist zerbrochen/ angeschlagen	Mīner tsahn-protayzer ist tsairbrokhen/ angeshlahgen
Can you fix it (temporarily)?	Können Sie sie (vorläufig) reparieren?	Kernen zee zee (fohrloyfikh) raypahreeren
You're hurting me	Sie tun mir weh	Zee toon meer vay
How much do I owe you?	Wieviel schulde ich Ihnen?	Veefeel shoolder ikh eenen
When should I come again?	Wann soll ich wiederkommen?	Van zoll ikh veeder-kommen
Please rinse your mouth	*Bitte spülen Sie den Mund aus	Bitter shpuilen zee dayn moont ows
I will X-ray your teeth	*Ich werde Ihre Zähne röntgen	Ikh vairder eerer tsehner rernt-gen

You have an abscess	*Sie haben ein Geschwür (einen Abszess)	Zee hahben īn geshvuir (īnen aptsess)
The nerve is exposed	*Der Nerv ist blossgelegt	Dair nairf ist blohs-gelaygt
This tooth can't be saved	*Dieser Zahn ist nicht zu retten	Deezair tsahn ist nikht tsoo retten

PROBLEMS & ACCIDENTS

Where's the police station?	**Wo ist die Polizeiwache?**	Voh ist dee pohleetsī-vakher
Call the police	**Rufen Sie die Polizei**	Roofen zee dee pohleetsī
It's urgent	**Es ist dringend**	Es ist dringent
There's a fire	**Es brennt**	Es brennt
A child has fallen in the water	**Ein Kind ist ins Wasser gefallen**	Īn kint ist ins vassair gefallen
A woman is drowning	**Eine Frau ist am Ertrinken**	Īner frow ist am air-trinken
My son/daughter is lost	**Mein Sohn/meine Tochter ist verschwunden**	Mīn zohn/mīner tokhtair ist fairshvoonden
Where is the British consulate?	**Wo ist das britische Konsulat?**	Voh ist das britisher konzoolaht
Please let the consulate know	**Bitte benachrichtigen Sie das Konsulat**	Bitter benakh-rikhtigen zee das konzoolaht

Our car has been broken into	Man ist in unseren Wagen eingebrochen	Man ist in oonzairen vahgen īngebrokhen
I've been robbed/ mugged	Man hat mich bestohlen/ überfallen	Man hat mikh beshtohlen/uibairfallen
My bag has been stolen	Man hat mir meine Tasche gestohlen	Man hat meer mīner tasher geshtohlen
I found this in the street	Ich habe dies auf der Strasse gefunden	Ikh hahber dees owf dair shtrahsser gefoonden
I have lost my luggage/passport/ travellers' cheques	Ich habe mein Gepäck/meinen Pass/meine Reiseschecks verloren	Ikh hahber mīn gepeck/ mīnen pas/mīner rīzer-sheks fairlohren
I have missed my train	Ich habe meinen Zug verpasst	Ikh hahber mīnen tsoog fairpasst
My luggage is on board	Mein Gepäck ist an Bord	Mīn gepeck ist an bort
Call a doctor	Rufen Sie einen Arzt	Roofen zee īnen artst
Call an ambulance	Rufen Sie einen Krankenwagen	Roofen zee īnen kranken-vahgen
There has been an accident	Ein Unfall hat sich ereignet	Īn oonfall hat zikh air-īgnet
He's badly hurt	Er ist schwer verletzt	Ayr ist shvayr fairletst
He has fainted	Er ist ohnmächtig geworden	Ayr ist ohn-mekhtikh gevorden
He's losing blood	Er verliert Blut	Avr fairleert bloot

Her arm is broken	Sie hat sich den Arm gebrochen	Zee hat zikh dayn arm gebrokhen
Please get some water a blanket some bandages	Bitte holen Sie etwas Wasser eine Decke Verbandszeug	Bitter hohlen zee etvas vassair īner decker fairbants-tsoyg
I've broken my glasses	Meine Brille ist kaputt	Mīner briller ist kapoot
I can't see	Ich kann nichts sehen	Ikh kan nikhts zayen
May I see your insurance certificate/driving licence	*Ich möchte Ihren Versicherungsschein/ Führerschein sehen	Ikh merkhter eeren fair-zikheroongs-shīn/ fuirairshīn zayen
Apply to the insurance company	*Wenden Sie sich an die Versicherungs-gesellschaft	Venden zee zikh an dee fair-zikheroongs-gezellshaft
Can you help me?	Können Sie mir helfen?	Kernen zee meer helfen
I didn't understand the sign	Ich habe das Schild nicht verstanden	Ikh hahber das shilt nikht fairshtanden
How much is the fine?	Wie hoch ist die Strafe?	Vee hohkh ist dee shtrahfer
What are the name and address of the owner?	Wie ist der Name und die Adresse des Besitzers?	Vee ist dair nahmer oont dee addresser des bezitsers
Are you willing to act as a witness?	Sind Sie bereit, als Zeuge aufzutreten?	Zint zee berīt als tsoyger owftsootrayten

Can I have your name and address please?	**Ihren Namen und Ihre Adresse, bitte**	Eeren **nahmen** oont eerer addresser bitter
I want a copy of the police report	**Ich möchte eine Kopie des Polizeiberichts**	Ikh **merkhter** īner kohpee des pohleetsī-berikhts
There's a bus strike/go slow	***Die Busfahrer sind in den Streik/ einen Bummelstreik getreten**	Dee **boos**-fahrer zint in dayn shtrīk/īnen **boommel**-shtrīk getrayten

TIME & DATES

TIME

What time is it?	Wie spät ist es?	Vee spayt ist es
It's one o'clock	Es ist ein Uhr	Es ist īn oor
two o'clock	zwei Uhr	tsvī oor
five past eight[1]	fünf (Minuten) nach acht	fuinf (minooten) nahkh akht
quarter past five	Viertel nach fünf	feertel nahkh fuinf
twenty-five past eight	fünf vor halb neun	fuinf for halb noyn
half past nine	halb zehn	halb tsayn
twenty-five to seven	fünf nach halb sieben	fuinf nahkh halb zeeben

---

1. The basic sequence is: five, ten, quarter *past*; ten, five *to half*; half *to next hour*; five, ten *past half*; quarter, ten, five *to next hour*.

twenty to three	**zwanzig vor drei**	tsvantsikh for drī
quarter to ten	**dreiviertel zehn**	drīfeertel tsayn
Second	**die Sekunde**	Zekoonder
Minute	**die Minute**	Meenooter
Hour	**die Stunde**	Shtoonder
It's early/late	**Es ist früh/spät**	Es ist fruih/shpayt
My watch is slow/fast	**Meine Uhr geht nach/vor**	Mīner oor gayt nahkh/fohr
The clock has stopped	**Die Uhr ist stehengeblieben**	Dee oor ist **shtay-engebleeben**
Sorry I'm late	**Entschuldigen Sie die Verspätung**	Ent-**shooldigen** zee dee fairshpaytoong

DATE

What's the date?	**Welches Datum ist heute?**	Velkhes dahtoom ist hoyter
It's 9th December	**Es ist der neunte Dezember**	Es ist dair **noynter** daytsember
We're leaving on 5th January	**Wir fahren am fünften Januar ab**	Veer fahren am **fuinften** yanooahr ap
We got here on 27th July	**Wir sind am siebenundzwanzigsten Juli angekommen**	Veer zint am zeeben-oont-tsvantseegsten yoolee angekommen

DAY

Morning	der Morgen	Morgen
this morning	heute Morgen	hoyter morgen
in the morning	am Morgen/ morgens	am morgen/morgens
Midday, noon	der Mittag	Mittahg
at noon	zu Mittag	tsoo mittahg
Afternoon	der Nachmittag	Nahkhmittahg
tomorrow afternoon	morgen nachmittag	morgen nahkhmittahg
Evening	der Abend	Ahbent
Midnight	Mitternacht	Mitter-nakt
Night	die Nacht	Nakht
tonight	heute abend	hoyter ahbent
last night	gestern abend	gestairn ahbent
Sunrise	der Sonnenaufgang	Zonnen-owfgang
Dawn	das Morgengrauen, der Tagesanbruch	Morgen-growen/ Tahges-anbrookh
Sunset	der Sonnen- untergang	Zonnen-oontairgang
Dusk, twilight	das Zwielicht	Tsveelikht
Today	heute	hoyter
Yesterday	gestern	gestairn
two days ago	vorgestern	forgestairn
Tomorrow	morgen	morgen
in two days	übermorgen	uibermorgen
in three days	in drei Tagen	in dri tahgen

WEEK

Monday	**Montag**	Mohntahg
Tuesday	**Dienstag**	Deenstahg
Wednesday	**Mittwoch**	Mitvokh
Thursday	**Donnerstag**	Donnairstahg
Friday	**Freitag**	Frītahg
Saturday	**Samstag/Sonnabend**	Zamstahg/Zonahbent
Sunday	**Sonntag**	Zontahg
on Tuesday	**(am) Dienstag**	(am) Deenstahg
on Sundays	**sonntags**	zontahgs
Fortnight	**zwei Wochen/**	tsvī vokhen/feertsayn
	vierzehn Tage	tahger

MONTH

January	**Januar**	Yanooahr
February	**Februar**	Febrooahr
March	**März**	Mairts
April	**April**	April
May	**Mai**	Mī
June	**Juni**	Yoonee
July	**Juli**	Yoolee
August	**August**	Owgoost
September	**September**	Septembair
October	**Oktober**	Octohbair

November	**November**	Nohvembair
December	**Dezember**	Daytsembair
in March	**im März**	im mairts

SEASON

Spring	**der Frühling/das Frühjahr**	Fruiling/fruiyahr
Summer	**der Sommer**	Zommair
Autumn	**der Herbst**	Hairbst
Winter	**der Winter**	Vintair
in spring	**im Frühjahr**	im fruiyahr
during the summer	**während des Sommers**	vairent des zommers

YEAR

This year	**dieses Jahr**	deezes yahr
Last year	**voriges/vergangenes Jahr**	foriges/fairgangenes yahr
Next year	**nächstes Jahr**	naikhstes yahr

PUBLIC HOLIDAYS

| 1 January | New Year's Day | **der Neujahrstag** |
| 6 January | Epiphany (Austria only) | **das Dreikönigsfest** |

	Good Friday	**der Karfreitag**
	Easter Monday	**der Ostermontag**
1 May	Mayday (not Switzerland)	**der Tag der Arbeit**
	Ascension Day	**der Himmelfahrtstag**
	Whit Monday	**der Pfingstmontag**
	Corpus Christi (Austria only)	**der Fronleichnam**
17 June	(Germany only)	**Siebzehnter Juni**
15 August	Ascension of the Virgin (Austria only)	**Mariä Himmelfahrt**
1 November	All Saints (Austria only)	**Allerheiligen**
16 November	(Germany only)	**Buss- und Bettag**
8 December	Conception Day (Austria only)	**die unbefleckte Empfängnis**
25 December	Christmas Day	**der (erste) Weihnachtstag**
26 December	Boxing Day	**der zweite Weihnachtstag**

NUMBERS

CARDINAL

0	**null**	nool
1	**eins**	īns
2	**zwei**	tsvī
3	**drei**	drī
4	**vier**	feer
5	**fünf**	fuinf
6	**sechs**	zeks
7	**sieben**	zeeben
8	**acht**	akht
9	**neun**	noyn
10	**zehn**	tsayn
11	**elf**	elf

12	zwölf	tsverlf
13	dreizehn	drītsayn
14	vierzehn	feertsayn
15	fünfzehn	fuinftsayn
16	sechzehn	zektsayn
17	siebzehn	zeebtsayn
18	achtzehn	akhtsayn
19	neunzehn	noyntsayn
20	zwanzig	tsvantsikh
21	einundzwanzig	īn-oont-tsvantsikh
22	zweiundzwanzig	tsvī-oont-tsvantsikh
30	dreissig	drīssikh
31	einunddreissig	īn-oont-drīssikh
32	zweiunddreissig	tsvī-oont-drīssikh
40	vierzig	feertsikh
41	einundvierzig	īn-oont-feertsikh
50	fünfzig	fuinftsikh
51	einundfünfzig	īn-oont-fuinftsikh
60	sechzig	zektsikh
61	einundsechzig	īne-oont-zektsiḳh
70	siebzig	zeebtsikh
71	einundsiebzig	īn-oont-zeebtsikh
80	achtzig	akhtsikh
81	einundachtzig	īn-oont-akhtsikh
90	neunzig	noyntsikh

91	**einundneunzig**	īn-oont-noyntsikh
100	**hundert**	hoondert
101	**hunderteins**	hoondertīns
200	**zweihundert**	tsvīhoondert
1,000	**tausend**	towzent
2,000	**zweitausend**	tsvītowzent
1,000,000	**eine Million**	iner meelyohn

ORDINAL

1st	**der erste**	airster
2nd	**zweite**	tsvīter
3rd	**dritte**	dritter
4th	**vierte**	feerter
5th	**fünfte**	fuinfter
6th	**sechste**	zekster
7th	**siebte**	zeebter
8th	**achte**	akhter
9th	**neunte**	noynter
10th	**zehnte**	tsaynter
11th	**elfte**	elfter
12th	**zwölfte**	tsverlfter
13th	**dreizehnte**	drītsaynter
14th	**vierzehnte**	feertsaynter
15th	**fünfzehnte**	fuinftsaynter
16th	**sechzehnte**	zektsaynter

17th	**siebzehnte**	zeebtsaynter
18th	**achtzehnte**	akhtsaynter
19th	**neunzehnte**	noyntsaynter
20th	**zwanzigste**	tsvantsigster
21st	**einundzwanzigste**	īn-oont-tsvantsikhster
30th	**dreissigste**	drīssikhster
40th	**vierzigste**	feertsikhster
50th	**fünfzigste**	fuinftsikhster
60th	**sechzigste**	zektsikhster
70th	**siebzigste**	zeebtsikhster
80th	**achtzigste**	akhtsikhster
90th	**neunzigste**	noyntsikhster
100th	**hundertste**	hoondertster
1000th	**tausendste**	towzentster
half	**(ein) halb**	halp
quarter	**(ein) Viertel**	feertel
three quarters	**dreiviertel**	drīfeertel
a third	**ein Drittel**	drittel
two thirds	**zwei Drittel**	tsvī drittel

WEIGHTS & MEASURES

DISTANCE

kilometres – miles

km	*miles or km*	miles	km	*miles or km*	miles
1.6	*1*	0.6	14.5	*9*	5.6
3.2	*2*	1.2	16.1	*10*	6.2
4.8	*3*	1.9	32.2	*20*	12.4
6.4	*4*	2.5	40.2	*25*	15.3
8	*5*	3.1	80.5	*50*	31.1
9.7	*6*	3.7	160.9	*100*	62.1
11.3	*7*	4.3	402.3	*250*	155.3
12.9	*8*	5.0	804.7	*500*	310.7

A rough way to convert from miles to km: divide by 5 and multiply by 8; from km to miles: divide by 8 and multiply by 5.

LENGTH AND HEIGHT

centimetres – inches

cm	inch or cm	inch	cm	inch or cm	inch
2.5	1	0.4	17.8	7	2.7
5.1	2	0.8	20.3	8	3.2
7.6	3	1.2	22.9	9	3.5
10.2	4	1.6	25.4	10	3.9
12.7	5	2.0	50.8	20	7.9
15.2	6	2.4	127	50	19.7

A rough way to convert from inches to cm: divide by 2 and multiply by 5; from cm to inches: divide by 5 and multiply by 2.

metres – feet

m	ft or m	ft	m	ft or m	ft
0.3	1	3.3	2.4	8	26.2
0.6	2	6.6	2.7	9	29.5
0.9	3	9.8	3	10	32.8
1.2	4	13.1	6.1	20	65.6
1.5	5	16.4	15.2	50	164
1.8	6	19.7	30.5	100	328.1
2.1	7	23	304.8	1,000	3,280

A rough way to convert from ft to m: divide by 10 and multiply by 3; from m to ft: divide by 3 and multiply by 10.

metres – yards

m	yds or m	yds	m	yds or m	yds
0.9	1	1.1	7.3	8	8.7
1.8	2	2.2	8.2	9	9.8
2.7	3	3.3	9.1	10	10.9
3.7	4	4.4	18.3	20	21.9
4.6	5	5.5	45.7	50	54.7
5.5	6	6.6	91.4	100	109.4
6.4	7	7.7	457.2	500	546.8

A rough way to convert from yds to m: subtract 10% from the number of yds; from m to yds: add 10% to the number of metres.

LIQUID MEASURES

litres – gallons

litres	galls or litres	galls	litres	galls or litres	galls
4.6	1	0.2	36.4	8	1.8
9.1	2	0.4	40.9	9	2.0
13.6	3	0.7	45.5	10	2.2
18.2	4	0.9	90.9	20	4.4
22.7	5	1.1	136.4	30	6.6
27.3	6	1.3	181.8	40	8.8
31.8	7	1.5	227.3	50	11

1 pint = 0.6 litre; 1 litre = 1.8 pint

A rough way to convert from galls to litres: divide by 2 and multiply by 9; from litres to galls: divide by 9 and multiply by 2.

WEIGHT

kilogrammes – pounds

kg	*lb or kg*	lb	kg	*lb or kg*	lb
0.5	*1*	2.2	3.2	*7*	15.4
0.9	*2*	4.4	3.6	*8*	17.6
1.4	*3*	6.6	4.1	*9*	19.8
1.8	*4*	8.8	4.5	*10*	22.0
2.3	*5*	11.0	9.1	*20*	44.1
2.7	*6*	13.2	22.7	*50*	110.2

A rough way to convert from lb to kg: divide by 11 and muliply by 5; from kg to lb: divide by 5 and multiply by 11.

grammes	oz	oz	grammes
100	3.5	2	56.7
250	8.8	4	114.3
500	17.6	8	228.6
1000 (1 kg)	35	16 (1 lb)	457.2

TEMPERATURE

centigrade (°C)	fahrenheit (°F)
°C	°F
– 10	14
– 5	23
0	32
5	41
10	50
15	59
20	68
25	77
30	86
35	95
37	98.4
38	100.5
39	102
40	104
100	212

To convert °F to °C: deduct 32, divide by 9, multiply by 5; to convert °C to °F: divide by 5, multiply by 9 and add 32.

BASIC GRAMMAR

There are four cases in German: NOMINATIVE (used for the subject or initiator of an action or speech), ACCUSATIVE (used for the person or thing directly affected by the action), DATIVE (used for the recipient), GENITIVE (used for the possessor). These cases are used for articles, nouns, pronouns and adjectives according to their position.

German also has three genders: masculine, feminine and neuter. They apply not only to living beings but also to inanimate objects: e.g. *der* Tisch (the table), *die* Tür (the door), *das* Bett (the bed). There are no clear rules for the use of the different genders. Similarly there are no precise easy rules on how to decline German nouns and these declensions have therefore been omitted.

DEFINITE ARTICLE

The definite article is declined as follows:

	Masculine	*Feminine*	*Neuter*	*Plural for all genders*	
Nom.	der	die	das	die	*the*
Acc.	den	die	das	die	*the*
Dat.	dem	der	dem	den	*to the*
Gen.	des	der	des	der	*of the*

The following words are declined in the same way as 'der, die, das':

Masculine	Feminine	Neuter	Plural for all genders	
dieser	diese	dieses	diese	*this*
jener	jene	jenes	jene	*that*
jeder	jede	jedes	jede	*every, each*
mancher	manche	manches	manche	*many (a)*
solcher	solche	solches	solche	*such (a)*
welcher?	welche?	welches?	welche?	*which (one)?*

INDEFINITE ARTICLE

The indefinite article is declined as follows:

	Masculine	Feminine	Neuter	
Nom.	ein	eine	ein	a
Acc.	einen	eine	ein	a
Dat.	einem	einer	einem	to a
Gen.	eines	einer	eines	of a

The following words are declined in the same way as 'ein, eine, ein' and, in addition, have a plural:

Masculine	Feminine	Neuter	Plural for all genders	
mein	meine	mein	meine	*my*
dein	deine	dein	deine	*your*
sein	seine	sein	seine	*his, its*
ihr	ihre	ihr	ihre	*her, their*
unser	uns(e)re	unser	uns(e)re	*our*
euer	eu(e)re	euer	eu(e)re	*your*
Ihr	Ihre	Ihr	Ihre	*your*
kein	keine	kein	keine	*no, not a*

Plural

Nom.	keine
Acc.	keine
Dat.	keinen
Gen.	keiner and, in the same way, the other words given above.

ADJECTIVES

The declension of adjectives is complex, but falls into a rigid pattern.
With the DEFINITE ARTICLE:

MASCULINE

	Singular		*Plural*
Nom.	der alte Mann	the old man	die alten Männer
Acc.	den alten Mann	the old man	die alten Männer
Dat.	dem alten Mann	to the old man	den alten Männern
Gen.	des alten Mannes	of the old man, the old man's	der alten Männer

FEMININE

	Singular		*Plural*
Nom.	die junge Frau	the young woman	die jungen Frauen
Acc.	die junge Frau	the young woman	die jungen Frauen
Dat.	der jungen Frau	to the young woman	den jungen Frauen
Gen.	der jungen Frau	of the young woman, the young woman's	der jungen Frauen

NEUTER

	Singular		*Plural*
Nom.	das kleine Kind	the small child	die kleinen Kinder
Acc.	das kleine Kind	the small child	die kleinen Kinder
Dat.	dem kleinen Kind	to the small child	den kleinen Kindern
Gen.	des kleinen Kindes	of the small child, the small child's	der kleinen Kinder

With the INDEFINITE ARTICLE:

MASCULINE

Nom.	ein alter Mann	an old man
Acc.	einen alten Mann	an old man
Dat.	einem alten Mann	to an old man
Gen.	eines alten Mannes	of an old man, an old man's

FEMININE

Nom.	eine junge Frau	a young woman
Acc.	eine junge Frau	a young woman
Dat.	einer jungen Frau	to a young woman
Gen.	einer jungen Frau	of a young woman, a young woman's

NEUTER

Nom.	ein kleines Kind	a small child
Acc.	ein kleines Kind	a small child
Dat.	einem kleinen Kind	to a small child
Gen.	eines kleinen Kindes	of a small child, a small child's

Without *either* article:

MASCULINE

	Singular		Plural
Nom.	süsser Wein	sweet wine	süsse Weine
Acc.	süssen Wein	sweet wine	süsse Weine
Dat.	süssem Wein	to sweet wine	süssen Weinen
Gen.	süssen Weins	of sweet wine	süsser Weine

FEMININE

	Singular		**Plural**
Nom.	alte Zeitung	old newspaper	alte Zeitungen
Acc.	alte Zeitung	old newspaper	alte Zeitungen
Dat.	alter Zeitung	to old newspaper	alten Zeitungen
Gen.	alter Zeitung	of old newspaper	alter Zeitungen

NEUTER

	Singular		**Plural**
Nom.	frisches Brot	fresh bread	frische Brote
Acc.	frisches Brot	fresh bread	frische Brote
Dat.	frischem Brot	to fresh bread	frischen Broten
Gen.	frischen Brot(e)s	of fresh bread	frischer Brote

PERSONAL PRONOUNS

Nominative		**Accusative**		**Dative**		**Genitive**	
ich	I	mich	me	mir	to me	meiner	mine
du	you	dich	you	dir	to you	deiner	yours
er	he	ihn	him	ihm	to him	seiner	his
sie	she	sie	her	ihr	to her	ihrer	hers
es	it	es	it	ihm	to it	seiner	its
wir	we	uns	us	uns	to us	unser	ours
ihr	you	euch	you	euch	to you	euer	yours
sie	they	sie	them	ihnen	to them	ihrer	theirs
Sie	you	Sie	you	Ihnen	to you	Ihrer	yours

'du' (singular) and 'ihr' (plural) are the familiar address used towards friends, relatives and children.

'Sie' (singular and plural) is the formal address used towards all other people. It is written with a capital 'S' when it means 'you' and small 's' when it means 'she', or 'they'.

PREPOSITIONS

The English meanings given in the list below are often only approximations, as prepositions in German are used to indicate a number of different meanings, e.g.

Ich wohn *bei* meinen Eltern = I am living *with* my parents.

Biegen Sie rechts *bei* den Verkehrsampeln ab = Turn right *at* the traffic lights.

With the **accusative** (i.e. they are always followed by the noun or pronoun in the accusative case):

durch	*through*
für	*for*
gegen	*against*
wider	*against*
ohne	*without*
um	*round, at (of time)*

With the **dative**:

mit	*with*
zu	*to*
nach	*to (a place), after, according to*
von	*of, from, by*
aus	*out of*
bei	*with, near, by*
seit	*since*
gegenüber	*opposite*
ausser	*except, besides*

With the *accusative or dative*:

in	*in, into, inside*
auf	*on, onto*
unter	*under*
über	*over, above*
an	*at, on, against*
vor	*before, in front of*
hinter	*behind*
zwischen	*between*
neben	*near, beside*

These prepositions are used with the *dative* when they indicate position or rest [e.g. Ich bin in dem Haus = I am in the house] or motion within a confined area [e.g. Ich gehe in dem Garten auf und ab = I am walking up and down in the garden]. They are used with the *accusative* if they indicate motion towards something or a change from one place to another [e.g. Ich gehe in das Haus = I go into the house].

With the *genitive*:

während	*during*
wegen	*because of*
trotz	*in spite of*
ausserhalb	*outside*
innerhalb	*inside*
statt/anstatt	*instead of*

INTERROGATIVE PRONOUNS

Nom.	wer?	*who?*	was?	*what?*
Acc.	wen?	*whom?*	was?	*what?*
Dat.	wem?	*to whom?*	wem?	*to what?*
Gen.	wessen?	*whose?*	wessen?	*of what?*

welcher? *which?* (see DEFINITE ARTICLE, p.206)

NEGATIVES

nicht	*not*
nie, niemals	*never*

The position of these words in a sentence depends very much on the stress the speaker wants to put on them. Generally, however, they stand in front of the word or idea to be negated.

VERBS

In German, as in English, there are certain basic verbs that one uses over and over again. These are:

Sein = to be

Present		*Future*	
ich bin	*I am*	ich werde sein	*I will be*
du bist	*you are*	du wirst sein	*you will be*
er	*he*	er	*he*
sie } ist	*she* } *is*	sie } wird sein	*she* } *will be*
es	*it*	es	*it*
wir sind	*we are*	wir werden sein	*we will be*
ihr seid	*you are*	ihr werdet sein	*you will be*
sie sind	*they are*	sie werden sein	*they will be*
Sie sind	*you are*	Sie werden sein	*you will be*

Perfect		*Imperfect*	
ich bin gewesen	*I have been*	ich war	*I was*
du bist gewesen	*you have been*	du warst	*you were*
er	*he*	er	*he*
sie } ist gewesen	*she* } *has been*	sie } war	*she* } *was*
es	*it*	es	*it*
wir sind gewesen	*we have been*	wir waren	*we were*

| sie sind gewesen | *they have been* | sie waren | *they were* |
| Sie sind gewesen | *you have been* | Sie waren | *you were* |

Haben = to have

Present		**Future**	
ich habe	*I have*	ich werde haben	*I will have*
du hast	*you have*	du wirst haben	*you will have*
er	*he*	er	*he*
sie } hat	*she } has*	sie } wird haben	*she } will have*
es	*it*	es	*it*
wir haben	*we have*	wir werden haben	*we will have*
ihr habt	*you have*	ihr werdet haben	*you will have*
sie haben	*they have*	sie werden haben	*they will have*
Sie haben	*you have*	Sie werden haben	*you will have*

Perfect		**Imperfect**	
ich habe gehabt	*I have had*	ich hatte	*I had*
du hast gehabt	*you have had*	du hattest	*you had*
er	*he*	er	*he*
sie } hat gehabt	*she } has had*	sie } hatte	*she } had*
es	*it*	es	*it*
wir haben gehabt	*we have had*	wir hatten	*we had*
ihr habt gehabt	*you have had*	ihr hattet	*you had*
sie haben gehabt	*they have had*	sie hatten	*they had*
Sie haben gehabt	*you have had*	Sie hatten	*you had*

Most German verbs are conjugated with 'haben' [e.g. Ich habe gesehen – I have seen]. The exceptions are the verb 'sein = to be' and all verbs of *motion* which are conjugated with 'sein' [e.g. Ich bin gelaufen – I have run, Ich bin gefahren – I have travelled].

AUXILIARY VERBS

These verbs are mostly used with the infinitive of another verb, and the latter always goes to the end of the sentence.

Dürfen = to be permitted (may)

Present	*Imperfect*
ich darf	ich durfte
du darfst	du durftest
er ⎫	er ⎫
sie ⎬ darf	sie ⎬ durfte
es ⎭	es ⎭
wir dürfen	wir durften
ihr dürft	ihr durftet
sie dürfen	sie durften
Sie dürfen	Sie durften

e.g. **Darf ich** rauchen? = May I smoke?

Können = to be able to (can)

Present	*Imperfect*
ich kann	ich konnte
du kannst	du konntest
er ⎫	er ⎫
sie ⎬ kann	sie ⎬ konnte
es ⎭	es ⎭
wir können	wir konnten
ihr könnt	ihr konntet
sie können	sie konnten
Sie können	Sie konnten

e.g. **Ich kann** Sie nicht verstehen = I cannot understand you.

Mögen = to have the inclination, liking (combined with the probability)

Present	*Imperfect*
ich mag	ich mochte
du magst	du mochtest
er ⎫	er ⎫
sie ⎬ mag	sie ⎬ mochte
es ⎭	es ⎭
wir mögen	wir mochten
ihr mögt	ihr mochtet
sie mögen	sie mochten
Sie mögen	Sie mochten

e.g. **Es mag** richtig sein = It may well be right.
Ich mag diesen Tee nicht = I don't like this tea.

Sollen = to have to (shall) (under order)

Present	*Imperfect*
ich soll	ich sollte
du sollst	du solltest
er ⎫	er ⎫
sie ⎬ soll	sie ⎬ sollte
es ⎭	es ⎭
wir sollen	wir sollten
ihr sollt	ihr solltet
sie sollen	sie sollten
Sie sollen	Sie sollten

e.g. **Er soll** zu mir kommen = He shall come to me.

Müssen = to have to (must)

Present	*Imperfect*
ich muss	ich musste
du musst	du musstest
er	er
sie } muss	sie } musste
es	es
wir müssen	wir mussten
ihr müsst	ihr musstet
sie müssen	sie mussten
Sie müssen	Sie mussten

e.g. **Sie müssen** um zehn Uhr hier sein = You have to be here at 10 o'clock.

Wollen = to want to, wish to (will)

Present	*Imperfect*
ich will	ich wollte
du willst	du wolltest
er	er
sie } will	sie } wollte
es	es
wir wollen	wir wollten
ihr wollt	ihr wolltet
sie wollen	sie wollten
Sie wollen	Sie wollten

e.g. **Ich will** mit dem Zug fahren = I want to go by train.

WEAK VERBS

A large group of German verbs – known as 'weak' – are conjugated by changing their endings, for instance:

Machen = to make, do

Present		*Future*	
ich mache	*I make*	ich werde machen	*I will make*
du machst	*you make*	du wirst machen	*you will make*
er	*he*	er	*he*
sie } macht	*she } makes*	sie } wird machen	*she } will make*
es	*it*	es	*it*
wir machen	*we make*	wir werden machen	*we will make*
ihr macht	*you make*	ihr werdet machen	*you will make*
sie machen	*they make*	sie werden machen	*they will make*
Sie machen	*you make*	Sie werden machen	*you will make*

Imperfect		*Perfect*	
ich machte	*I made*	ich habe gemacht	*I have made*
du machtest	*you made*	du hast gemacht	*you have made*
er	*he*	er	*he*
sie } machte	*she } made*	sie } hat gemacht	*she } has made*
es	*it*	es	*it*
wir machten	*we made*	wir haben gemacht	*we have made*
ihr machtet	*you made*	ihr habt gemacht	*you have made*
sie machten	*they made*	sie haben gemacht	*they have made*
Sie machten	*you made*	Sie haben gemacht	*you have made*

STRONG VERBS

However, many of the verbs in this phrase book can be grouped together as 'strong' verbs which means their form changes more drastically in different tenses.

Sprechen = to talk, speak

Present		*Future*	
ich spreche	*I speak*	ich werde sprechen	*I will speak*
du sprichst	*you speak*	du wirst sprechen	*you will speak*
er	*he*	er	*he*
sie } spricht	*she } speaks*	sie } wird sprechen	*she } will speak*
es	*it*	es	*it*
wir sprechen	*we speak*	wir werden sprechen	*we will speak*
ihr sprecht	*you speak*	ihr werdet sprechen	*you will speak*
sie sprechen	*they speak*	sie werden sprechen	*they will speak*
Sie sprechen	*you speak*	Sie werden sprechen	*you will speak*

Imperfect		*Perfect*	
ich sprach	*I spoke*	ich habe gesprochen	*I have spoken*
du sprachst	*you spoke*	du hast gesprochen	*you have spoken*
er	*he*	er	*he*
sie } sprach	*she } spoke*	sie } hat gesprochen	*she } has spoken*
es	*it*	es	*it*
wir sprachen	*we spoke*	wir haben gesprochen	*we have spoken*
ihr spracht	*you spoke*	ihr habt gesprochen	*you have spoken*
sie sprachen	*they spoke*	sie haben gesprochen	*they have spoken*
Sie sprachen	*you spoke*	Sie haben gesprochen	*you have spoken*

A list of the most common 'strong' verbs is given below:

Infinitive	*3rd person singular present*	*Imperfect*	*Past participle*	
beginnen	beginnt	begann	begonnen	*to begin*
biegen	biegt	bog	gebogen	*to bend, turn*
bitten	bittet	bat	gebeten	*to entreat, beg (... um = ask for)*
bleiben	bleibt	blieb	geblieben	*to remain, stay*

bringen	bringt	brachte	gebracht	*to bring*
denken	denkt	dachte	gedacht	*to think*
empfehlen	empfiehlt	empfahl	empfohlen	*to recommend*
essen	isst	ass	gegessen	*to eat*
fahren	fährt	fuhr	gefahren	*to drive, travel*
fangen	fängt	fing	gefangen	*to catch*
finden	findet	fand	gefunden	*to find*
fliegen	fliegt	flog	geflogen	*to fly*
geben	gibt	gab	gegeben	*to give*
gefallen	es gefällt (mir)	gefiel	gefallen	*to like*
gehen	geht	ging	gegangen	*to go*
geschehen	es geschieht	geschah	geschehen	*to happen*
halten	hält	hielt	gehalten	*to hold*
heissen	heisst	hiess	geheissen	*to be called*
helfen	hilft	half	geholfen	*to help*
kennen	kennt	kannte	gekannt	*to know*
kommen	kommt	kam	gekommen	*to come*
lassen	lässt	liess	gelassen	*to leave, let*
laufen	läuft	lief	gelaufen	*to run*
liegen	liegt	lag	gelegen	*to lie*
nehmen	nimmt	nahm	genommen	*to take*
rufen	ruft	rief	gerufen	*to call*
schliessen	schliesst	schloss	geschlossen	*to close, shut*
schreiben	schreibt	schrieb	geschrieben	*to write*
sehen	sieht	sah	gesehen	*to see*
sitzen	sitzt	sass	gesessen	*to sit*
sprechen	spricht	sprach	gesprochen	*to speak, talk*
stehen	steht	stand	gestanden	*to stand*
tragen	trägt	trug	getragen	*to carry, wear*
treffen	trifft	traf	getroffen	*to meet*
treten	tritt	trat	getreten	*to step*
trinken	trinkt	trank	getrunken	*to drink*
tun	tut	tat	getan	*to do, make*

vergessen	vergisst	vergass	vergessen	*to forget*
verlieren	verliert	verlor	verloren	*to lose*
verstehen	versteht	verstand	verstanden	*to understand*
werden	wird	wurde	geworden	*to become*
wissen	weiss	wusste	gewusst	*to know*

SEPARABLE VERBS

There are some verbs in German which, by having a prefix added, modify their meaning:

e.g.

kommen	*to come*
ankommen	*to arrive*
fangen	*to catch*
anfangen	*to start*
fahren	*to travel, drive*
abfahren	*to depart*

When conjugated the prefix is separated from the verb in the present and imperfect and put at the end of the sentence.

e.g. abfahren: Der Zug *fährt* bald *ab* = The train leaves soon.

VOCABULARY

Various groups of specialized words are given elsewhere in this book and these words are not usually repeated in the vocabulary:

A

a, an	**ein/eine/ein**	īn/īner/īn
abbey	**die Abtei**	aptī
able (to be)	**können**	kernen
about	**ungefähr**	oongefair
above	**über**	uiber
abroad	**im Ausland**	im owslant
accept (to)	**annehmen**	an-naymen
accident	**der Unfall**	oonfall
accommodation	**die Unterkunft**	oontair-koonft
ache (to)	**schmerzen**	shmairtsen
acquaintance	**der Bekannte**	bekanter
across	**über, jenseits**	uiber, yaynzītes
act (to)	**handeln**	handeln
act *stage*	**spielen**	shpeelen
add (to)	**hinzufügen**	hintsoofuigen
address	**die Adresse**	adresser
admire (to)	**bewundern**	bevoondairn
admission	**der Eintritt**	īn-tritt
adventure	**das Abenteuer**	ahbentoyair
advertisement	**die Anzeige**	antsīger
advice	**der Rat**	raht
aeroplane	**das Flugzeug**	flooktsoyg
afford (to)	**sich** (*dat*) **leisten**	zeekh līsten
afraid	**ängstlich**	engstlikh
after	**nach**	nahkh

afternoon	der Nachmittag	nahkh-mittakh
again	wieder	veedair
against	gegen/wider	gaygen/vidair
age	das Alter	alter
agree (to)	zustimmen	tsooshtimmen
ahead	vorn	forn
air	die Luft	looft
air-conditioning	die Klimaanlage	kleema-anlahger
alarm clock	der Wecker	vekair
alcoholic *drink*	alkoholisch	alkoh-hohleesh
alike	ähnlich	aynlikh
alive	lebendig	lebendikh
all	alles	alles
allow (to)	erlauben	airlowben
all right	in Ordnung	in ordnoong
almost	fast	fast
alone	allein	allīn
along	entlang	entlang
already	schon	shohn
also	auch	owkh
alter (to)	ändern	endairn
alternative	die Alternative	altairnahteever
although	obgleich	opglīkh
always	immer	immer
ambulance	der Krankenwagen	kranken-vahgen
America	Amerika	amaireekah

American *adj*	**amerikanisch**	amaireekahnish
American *noun*	**der Amerikaner**	amaireekahnair
among	**zwischen/bei**	tsvishen/bī
amuse (to)	**amüsieren**	amuizeeren
amusement park	**der Vergnügungspark**	fairgnuigoongspahrk
amusing	**amüsant**	amuizant
ancient	**sehr alt**	zayr alt
and	**und**	oont
angry	**zornig**	tsornikh
animal	**das Tier**	teer
anniversary	**die Jahresfeier**	yahresfī-er
annoyed	**geärgert/verärgert**	ge-airgert/fair-airgert
another	**ein anderer**	īn andairair
answer	**die Antwort**	antvort
answer (to)	**antworten**	antvorten
antique	**die Antike**	anteeker
antique shop	**der Antiquitätenladen**	anteekveetayten-lahden
any	**irgendein**	eergent-īn
anyone	**irgendeiner**	eergent-īnair
anything	**irgend etwas**	eergent etvas
anyway	**jedenfalls**	yayden-fals
anywhere	**irgendwo**	eergent-voh
apartment	**die Wohnung**	vohnoong
apologize (to)	**sich entschuldigen**	zikh entshooldigen
appetite	**der Appetit**	appeteet

appointment	die Verabredung	fairapraydoong
architect	der Architekt	arkheetekt
architecture	die Architektur	arkheetektoor
area	das Gebiet	gebeet
area code	die Vorwahlnummer	fohrvahlnoomair
arm	der Arm	arm
armchair	der Lehnstuhl	laynshtool
army	das Heer/die Armee	hayr/armay
around	rings herum	rings hairoom
arrange (to)	festsetzen	festzet-tsen
arrival	die Ankunft	ankoonft
arrive (to)	ankommen	ankommen
art	die Kunst	koonst
art gallery	die Kunstgalerie	koonst-galairee
artificial	künstlich	kuinstlikh
artist	der Künstler	kuinstlair
as	wie	vee
as much as	soviel wie	zohfeel vee
as soon as	sobald	zohbalt
as well/also	auch	owkh
ashtray	der Aschenbecher	ashen-bekher
ask (to)	fragen	frahgen
asleep	eingeschlafen	īn-geshlahfen
at	an/zu/bei/um	an/tsoo/bī/oom
at last	endlich	entlikh
at once	sofort	zohfort

English	German	Pronunciation
atmosphere	**die Atmosphäre**	atmohsfairer
attention	**die Aufmerksamkeit**	owfmairkzamkīt
attractive	**reizend**	rītsent
auction	**die Auktion**	owktseeohn
audience	**die Zuhörer**	tsooher-rer
aunt	**die Tante**	tanter
Australia	**Australien**	owstrahleeyen
Australian	**australisch**	owstrahlish
Austria	**Österreich**	erstairīkh
Austrian	**österreichisch**	erstairīkhish
author	**der Schriftsteller/ Autor**	shrift-shtellair/owtor
autumn	**der Herbst**	hairpst
available	**vorhanden**	forhanden
avalanche	**die Lawine**	lahveener
avenue	**die Allee**	allay
average	**durchschnittlich**	doorkh-shnitlikh
avoid (to)	**vermeiden**	fairmīden
awake	**wach**	vakh
away	**weg**	vek
awful	**schrecklich**	shreklikh

B

English	German	Pronunciation
baby	**das Baby**	baybee
baby food	**die Babynahrung**	baybeenahroong

baby sitter	der (die) Babysitter(in)	baybeesittair
bachelor	der Junggeselle	yoong-gezeler
back	zurück	tsooruik
bad	schlecht	shlekht
bag	die Tasche	tasher
baggage	das Gepäck	gepeck
baggage cart	der Gepäckwagen	gepeck-vahgen
baggage check	die Gepäckkontrolle	gepeck-kontroller
bait	der Köder	kerdair
balcony	der Balkon	balkohn
ball *sport*	der Ball	bal
ballet	das Ballett	balet
balloon	der Ballon	ballon
band *music*	die Kapelle	kapeller
bank	die Bank	bank
bank account	das Konto	kontoh
bare	nackt	nakt
barn	die Scheune	shoyner
basket	der Korb	korp
bath	das Bad	baht
bathe (to)	baden	bahden
bath essence	der Badezusatz	bahdertsoozats
bathing cap	die Bademütze	bahder-muitser
bathing costume	der Badeanzug	bahder-antsook
bathing trunks	die Badehose	bahder-hohzer

bathroom	**das Badezimmer**	**bah**der-tsimmer
battery	**die Batterie**	batteree
bay	**die Bucht**	bookht
be (to)	**sein**	zīn
beach	**der Strand**	shtrant
beard	**der Bart**	bahrt
beautiful	**schön**	shern
because	**weil**	vīl
become (to)	**werden**	vairden
bed	**das Bett**	bet
bedroom	**das Schlafzimmer**	shlahf-tsimmer
before	**vor/bevor**	fohr/be-**fohr**
begin (to)	**beginnen**	beginnen
beginning	**der Anfang**	anfang
behind	**hinter**	hintair
believe (to)	**glauben**	glow**ben**
bell	**die Glocke**	glocker
belong (to)	**gehören**	geher-ren
below	**unter**	oontair
belt	**der Gürtel**	guirtell
bench	**die Bank**	bank
bend (to)	**biegen**	beegen
beneath	**unter**	oontair
berth	**das Bett**	bet
beside	**neben**	nayben
besides	**ausserdem**	owsairdaym

best	das Beste	bester
bet	die Wette	vetter
better	besser	besser
between	zwischen	tsvishen
bicycle	das Fahrrad	fahr-raht
big	gross	grohs
bill	die Rechnung	rekhnoong
binoculars	das Fernglas	fernglahs
bird	der Vogel	fohgel
birthday	der Geburtstag	geboortstahg
bite (to)	beissen	bīsen
bitter	herb	herp
blanket	die Wolldecke	volldecker
bleed (to)	bluten	blooten
blind	blind	bleent
blister	die Blase	blahzer
blond	blond	blont
blood	das Blut	bloot
blouse	die Bluse	bloozer
blow (to)	blasen	blahzen
(on) board	an Bord	an bort
boarding house	die Pension	pensyohn
boat	das Boot/Schiff	boht/sheef
body	der Körper	kerper
bolt	der Türriegel	tuir-reegel
bone	der Knochen	knokhen

book	das Buch	bookh
book (to)	buchen	bookhen
boot	der Stiefel	shteefel
border	die Grenze	grentser
bored	gelangweilt	gelangvīlt
boring	langweilig	langvīlikh
borrow (to)	borgen	borgen
both	beide	bīder
bother (to) *annoy*	behelligen	behelleegen
bottle	die Flasche	flasher
bottle opener	der Flaschenöffner	flashen-erfnair
bottom	der Boden	boh-den
bowl	die Schüssel	shuissel
bow tie	die Fliege	fleeger
box *container*	die Schachtel	shakhtel
box *theatre*	die Loge	lohjer
box office	die Kasse	kasser
boy	der Junge	yoonger
bracelet	das Armband	armbant
braces	der Hosenträger	hohzen-trayger
brain	das Gehirn	geheern
branch	der Zweig	tsvīg
brand	die Marke	marker
brassière	der Büstenhalter/BH	buistenhaltair/beha
break (to)	brechen	brekhen
breakfast	das Frühstück	frui-shtuik

breathe (to)	**atmen**	ahtmen
brick	**der Backstein**	bakshtīn
bridge	**die Brücke**	bruiker
briefs	**der Schlüpfer**	shluipfair
bright	**leuchtend/hell**	loykhtent/hell
bring (to)	**bringen**	bringen
British	**britisch**	british
broken	**gebrochen/ zerbrochen**	gebrokhen/tsair-brokhen
brooch	**die Brosche**	brosher
brother	**der Bruder**	brooder
bruise (to)	**quetschen**	kvetshen
brush	**die Bürste**	buirster
brush (to)	**bürsten**	buirsten
bucket	**der Eimer**	īmer
buckle	**die Schnalle**	shnaller
build (to)	**bauen**	bowen
building	**das Gebäude**	geboyder
bundle	**das Bündel**	buindel
burn (to)	**brennen**	brennen
burst (to)	**bersten**	bairsten
bus	**der Bus**	boos
bus stop	**die Bushaltestelle**	boos-halter-shteller
business	**das Geschäft**	gesheft
busy	**beschäftigt**	besheftikht
but	**aber**	ahbair

butterfly	**der Schmetterling**	shmettair-ling
button	**der Knopf**	k-nopf
buy (to)	**kaufen**	kowfen
by	**von/bei**	fon/bī

C

cabin	**die Kabine**	kabeener
calculator	**der Rechner**	rekhnair
calendar	**der Kalender**	kalendair
call *telephone*	**der Anruf**	anroof
call *visit*	**der Besuch**	bezookh
call (to) *summon*	**rufen**	roofen
call (to) *name*	**nennen**	nennen
call (to) *telephone*	**anrufen**	anroofen
call (to) *visit*	**besuchen**	bezookhen
calm	**ruhig**	roo-ikh
camera	**die Kamera/der Fotoapparat**	kamerah/fohtoh-appa-raht
camp (to)	**zelten**	tselten
camp site	**der Zeltplatz**	tselt-plats
can *to be able*	**können**	kernen
can *tin*	**die Dose**	dozer
Canada	**Kanada**	kanada
Canadian	**kanadisch**	kanahdish
cancel (to)	**abbestellen**	ap-beshtellen
candle	**die Kerze**	kairtser

canoe	das Kanu	kanoo
can opener	der Dosenöffner	dohzen-erfnair
cap	die Mütze	muitser
capable	fähig	fayh-ikh
capital city	die Hauptstadt	howpt-shtaht
car	das Auto	owtoh
carafe	die Karaffe	karaffer
caravan	der Wohnwagen	vohnvahgen
card	die Karte	karter
care (to)	sorgen	zorgen
careful	sorgsam	zorgzahm
careless	unachtsam	oonakhtzahm
caretaker	der Wärter	vairtair
car park	der Parkplatz	parkplats
carpet	der Teppich	teppikh
carry (to)	tragen	trahgen
cash	das Bargeld	bahrgelt
cash (to)	einlösen	īn-lerzen
cashier	der Kassierer	kaseerair
casino	das Kasino	kazeenoh
cassette	die Kassette	kahsetter
cassette recorder	der Kassettenrecorder	kahsetten-raykordair
castle	das Schloss/die Burg	shloss/boorg
cat	die Katze	katser
catalogue	der Katalog	katalohg

catch (to)	**fangen**	fangen
cathedral	**der Dom**	dohm
catholic	**katholisch**	katohleesh
cause	**der Grund**	groont
cave	**die Höhle**	herler
cement	**der Zement**	tsayment
central	**zentral**	tsentrahl
centre	**das Zentrum**	tsentroom
century	**das Jahrhundert**	yahr-hoondairt
ceremony	**die Zeremonie**	tsay-remohnee
certain	**sicher**	zeekhair
certainly	**gewiss**	geviss
chain *jewellery*	**die Kette**	ketter
chair	**der Stuhl**	shtool
chambermaid	**das Zimmermädchen**	tsimmer-maytkhen
chance	**die Möglichkeit**	mergleekh-kīt
(by) chance	**(durch) Zufall**	tsoofal
(small) change	**das Kleingeld**	klīn-gelt
change (to)	**einwechseln**	īn-vekseln
chapel	**die Kapelle**	kahpeller
charge	**der Preis**	prīs
charge (to)	**berechnen**	berekhnen
cheap	**billig**	billikh
check (to)	**nachrechnen**	nakh-rekhnen
chef	**der Chef**	shef
cheque	**der Scheck**	sheck

chess	**Schach**	shakh
chess set	**das Schachspiel**	shakh-shpeel
child	**das Kind**	kint
chill (to)	**kühlen**	kuilen
china	**das Porzellan**	portselahn
choice	**die Wahl**	vahl
choose (to)	**(aus)wählen**	(ows)vaylen
church	**die Kirche**	keerkher
cigarette case	**das Zigarettenetui**	tseegahretten-aytvee
cine camera	**die Filmkamera**	filmkamerah
cinema	**das Kino**	keenoh
circus	**der Zirkus**	tseerkoos
city	**die (Gross)stadt**	(grohs)shtat
class	**die Klasse**	klasser
clean	**rein**	rīn
clean (to)	**reinigen**	rīn-eegen
cleansing cream	**die Reinigungscreme**	rīneegoongs-kraymer
clear	**klar**	klahr
clerk	**der Beamte**	beamter
cliff	**die Klippe**	klipper
climb (to)	**besteigen**	beshtīgen
cloakroom	**die Toilette**	twaletter
clock	**die Uhr**	oor
close (to)	**schliessen**	shleessen
closed	**geschlossen**	geshlossen
cloth	**der Stoff**	shtof

clothes	die Kleider	klīdair
cloud	die Wolke	volker
coach	der Autobus	owtohboos
coast	die Küste	kuister
coat	der Mantel	mantel
coathanger	der (Kleider)bügel	(klīdair)buigel
coin	die Münze	muintser
cold	kalt	kalt
cold (to have)	einen Schnupfen haben	shnoop-feu hah-ben
collar	der Kragen	krahgen
collect (to)	sammeln	zammeln
colour	die Farbe	farber
comb	der Kamm	kam
come (to)	kommen	kommen
come in (to)	hereinkommen	hairīn-kommen
comfortable	bequem	bekvaym
common	allgemein	algemīn
compact disc	Compact disc (CD)	kompakt disk (tsay day)
company	die Gesellschaft	gezelshaft
compartment	das Abteil	aptīl
compass	der Kompass	kompas
compensation	die Abfindung	apfindoong
complain (to)	sich beschweren	zikh beshvairen
complaint	die Beschwerde	beshvairder
complete	komplett	komplet

completely	ganz	gants
conductor *bus*	der Schaffner	shaffnair
computer	der Computer	kompyootair
concert	das Konzert	kontsert
concert hall	die Konzerthalle	kontsairt-haller
concrete	konkret	konkrayt
condition	der Zustand	tsooshtant
conductor *bus*	der Schaffner	shaffnair
conductor *orchestra*	der Dirigent	deereegent
congratulations	herzlichen Glückwunsch	hairtsleekhen gluikvoonsh
connect (to)	verbinden	fairbinden
connection *train, etc.*	der Anschluss	anshloos
consul	der Konsul	konzool
consulate	das Konsulat	konzoolaht
contact lens	die Kontaktlinse	kontaktlinzer
contain (to)	enthalten	enthalten
contraceptive	das empfängnis-verhütende Mittel	empfengnis-fairhuitende mittel
convenient	günstig	guinstikh
conversation	die Unterhaltung	oontairhaltoong
cook	der Koch/die Köchin	kokh/kerkhin
cook (to)	kochen	kokhen
cool	kühl	kuil
copy	das Exemplar/die Kopie	eksemplahr/kohpee
copy (to)	kopieren	kohpeeren
cork	der Korken	korken

corkscrew	der Korkenzieher	korken-tseeyer
corner	die Ecke	ecker
correct	richtig	rikhtikh
corridor	der Korridor	korreedohr
cosmetics	die Kosmetikartikel	kosmaytik-artikel
cost	der Preis	prīs
cost (to)	kosten	kosten
costume jewellery	der Modeschmuck	mohder-shmook
cotton	die Baumwolle	bowmvoller
cotton wool	die Watte	vatter
couchette	der Liegeplatz	leeger-plats
count (to)	zählen	tsaylen
country	das Land	lant
couple	das Paar	pahr
course *dish*	das Gericht	gereekht
courtyard	der Hof	hohf
cousin	der Vetter/die Kusine	fet-tair/koozeener
cover	die Decke	decker
cover (to)	bedecken	bedecken
cow	die Kuh	koo
crash *collision*	der Zusammenstoß	tsoozammen-shtohs
crease	die Falte	falter
credit	das Guthaben/der Kredit	goot-hahben/kraydeet
credit card	die Kreditkarte	kraydeet-karter
crew	die Besatzung	bezatsoong

cross	**das Kreuz**	kroyts
cross (to)	**hinübergehen**	hinuibair-gayen
cross country skiing	**der (Ski)Langlauf**	(shee)**langlowf**
crossroads	**die Kreuzung**	kroy-tsoong
crowd	**die Menge**	menger
crowded	**voll**	foll
cry (to)	**schreien**	shri-en
crystal	**der Kristall**	kristal
cufflinks	**die Manschetten-knöpfe**	manshetten-knerpfer
cup	**die Tasse**	tasser
cupboard	**der Schrank**	shrank
cure (to)	**heilen**	hīlen
curious	**neugierig**	noygeerikh
curl	**die Locke**	loker
current	**die Strömung**	shtrermoong
curtain	**der Vorhang**	fohrhang
curve	**die Kurve**	koorver
cushion	**das Kissen**	kissen
customs	**der Zoll**	tsoll
customs officer	**der Zollbeamte**	tsoll-be-amter
cut	**der Schnitt**	shnit
cut (to)	**schneiden**	shnīden
cycling	**das Radfahren**	rat-fahren
cyclist	**der Radfahrer**	rat-fahrair

D

daily	**täglich**	tayglikh
damaged	**beschädigt**	beshaydikht
damp	**feucht**	foykht
dance	**der Tanz**	tants
danger	**die Gefahr**	gefahr
dangerous	**gefährlich**	gefairlikh
dark	**dunkel**	doonkel
date	**das Datum**	dahtoom
date *appointment*	**die Verabredung**	fairapraydoong
daughter	**die Tochter**	tokhter
day	**der Tag**	tahg
dead	**tot**	toht
deaf	**taub**	towb
dealer	**der Händler**	hentlair
dear *expensive*	**teuer**	toyer
decanter	**die Karaffe**	karaffer
decide (to)	**entscheiden**	entshīden
deck	**das Deck**	deck
deckchair	**der Liegestuhl**	leeger-shtool
declare (to) *customs*	**verzollen**	fairtsollen
declare (to)	**erklären**	airklayren
deep	**tief**	teef
delay	**die Verzögerung**	fair-tsergeroong
deliver (to)	**austragen**	owstrahgen
delivery	**die Austragung**	owstrahgoong

demi-pension	das Zimmer mit halber Verpflegung	tsimmer mit halbair fairpflaygoong
dentist	der Zahnarzt	tsahnartst
deodorant	das Deodorant	dayodorant
depart (to)	abfahren	apfahren
department	die Abteilung	aptīl-oong
department store	das Warenhaus	vahrenhows
departure	die Abfahrt	apfahrt
dessert	der Nachtisch	nakh-tish
detour	der Umweg	oomvaykh
dial (to)	wählen	vaylen
dialling code	die Vorwahlnummer	fohrvahlnoomair
diamond	der Diamant	deeahmant
dice	der Würfel	vuirfel
dictionary	das Wörterbuch	vertairbookh
diet	die Diät	dee-ayt
diet (to)	Diät halten	dee-ayt halten
different	verschieden	fairsheeden
difficult	schwierig	shveerikh
dine (to)	speisen/essen	spīzen/essen
dining room	der Speisesaal	shpīzerzahl
dinner	das Abendessen	ahbent-essen
dinner jacket	die Smokingjacke	smohking-yaker
direct	direkt	deerekt
direction	die Richtung	reekhtoong
dirty	schmutzig	shmootsikh

disappointed	enttäuscht	ent-toysht
discotheque	die Diskothek	diskohtayk
discount	der Rabatt	rahbat
dish	die Schüssel	shuissel
disinfectant	das Desinfiziermittel	dayzinfeetseermittel
distance	die Entfernung	entfairnoong
disturb (to)	stören	shteren
ditch	der Graben	grahben
dive (to)	tauchen	towkhen
diving board	das Sprungbrett	sproongbret
divorced	geschieden	gesheeden
do (to)	tun	toon
dock (to)	anlegen	anlaygen
doctor	der Arzt	ahrtst
dog	der Hund	hoont
doll	die Puppe	pooper
door	die Tür	tuir
double	doppelt	doppelt
double bed	das Doppelbett	doppel-bet
double room	das Doppelzimmer	doppel-tsimmer
down	hinunter	hinoontair
downstairs	unten	oonten
dozen	das Dutzend	dootsent
draughty	zugig	tsoogikh
draw (to)	zeichnen	tsīkhnen
drawer	die Schublade	shoob-lahder

drawing	**die Zeichnung**	tsīkhnoong
dream	**der Traum**	trowm
dress	**das Kleid**	klīt
dressing-gown	**der Morgenrock**	morgenrock
dressmaker	**die Damenschneiderin**	dahmen-shnīderin
drink (to)	**trinken**	treenken
drinking water	**das Trinkwasser**	treenkvassair
drive (to)	**fahren**	fahren
driver	**der Fahrer**	fahrer
driving licence	**der Führerschein**	fuihrer-shīn
drop (to)	**fallen lassen**	fallen lassen
drunk	**betrunken**	betroonken
dry *adj.*	**trocken**	trocken
during	**während**	vayrent
duvet	**die Daunendecke**	downendeker
dye	**der Farbstoff**	farpshtoff

E

each	**jeder/-e/-es**	yaydair/yayder/yaydes
early	**früh**	frui
earrings	**die Ohrringe**	ohr-ringer
east	**der Osten**	osten
Easter	**Ostern**	ohstairn
easy	**leicht**	līkht
eat (to)	**essen**	essen

edge	der Rand	rant
EEC	die EWG	ay-vay-gay
eiderdown	das Federbett	fayderbet
elastic	das Gummiband	goomeebant
electric light bulb	die Glühbirne	gluibeerner
electric point	die Steckdose	shteckdozer
electricity	die Elektrizität	aylektreetsitayt
elevator	der Fahrstuhl	fahr-shtool
embarrass (to)	in Verlegenheit setzen	in fairlaygenhīt zetsen
embassy	die Botschaft	bohtshaft
emergency exit	der Notausgang	noht-owsgang
empty	leer	layr
end	das Ende	ender
engaged *people*	verlobt	fairlohbt
engaged *telephone*	besetzt	bezetst
engine	der Motor	mohtor
England	England	englant
English	englisch	english
Englishman	der Engländer	englendair
enjoy (to)	geniessen	geneessen
enough	genug	genoog
enquiries	die Auskunft	owskoonft
enter (to)	hineintreten	hinīn-trayten
entrance	der Eingang	īn-gang
entrance fee	die Eintrittsgebühr	īntrits-gebuihr

envelope	der (Brief)umschlag	(breef)oomshlahg
equipment	die Ausrüstung	ows-ruistoong
escalator	die Rolltreppe	rol-trepper
escape (to)	entkommen	entkommen
estate agent	der Hausmakler	hows-mahklair
Europe	Europa	oyrohpah
even *not odd*	gerade	gerahder
evening	der Abend	ahbent
event	der Vorfall	fohrfal
ever	immer	immer
every	jeder/-e/-es	yaydair/yayder/yaydes
everybody	jedermann	yaydairman
everything	alles	alles
everywhere	überall	uiberal
example	das Beispiel	bīshpeel
excellent	ausgezeichnet	owsgetsīkhnet
except	ausser	owssair
excess	das Übermass	uibermahss
exchange bureau	die Wechselstube	vekselshtoober
exchange rate	der Wechselkurs	vekselkoors
excursion	der Ausflug	owsfloog
excuse	die Entschuldigung	entshooldeegoong
exhausted	erschöpft	airsherpft
exhibition	die Ausstellung	owsshtelloong
exit	der Ausgang	owsgang
expect (to)	erwarten	airvarten

expensive	**teuer**	toyer
explain (to)	**erklären**	airklayren
express	**die Eilpost**	īl-post
express train	**der Schnellzug**	shneltsoog
extra	**zusätzlich**	tsoozetslikh

F

fabric	**der Stoff**	shtof
face	**das Gesicht**	gezikht
face cloth	**der Waschlappen**	vashlappen
face cream	**die Gesichtscreme**	gezikhts-kraymer
face powder	**der (Gesichts)Puder**	(gezikhts)poodair
fact	**die Tatsache**	tahtzakher
factory	**die Fabrik**	fabreek
fade (to)	**verblassen**	fairblassen
faint (to)	**in Ohnmacht fallen**	in ohnmakht fallen
fair	**blond**	blont
fair *fête*	**der Jahrmarkt**	yahrmarkt
fall (to)	**fallen**	fallen
family	**die Familie**	fameelyer
far	**weit**	vīt
fare	**das Fahrgeld**	fahrgelt
farm	**der Bauernhof**	bowernhohf
farmer	**der Bauer**	bower
farmhouse	**das Bauernhaus**	bowairn-hows
farther	**weiter**	vīt-air

fashion	die Mode	mohder
fast	schnell	shnell
fat	dick	dick
father	der Vater	fahtair
fault	der Fehler	fayler
fear	die Angst	angst
feed (to)	ernähren	airnayren
feeding bottle	die (Baby)Flasche	(baybee)flasher
feel (to)	fühlen	fuilen
felt-tip pen	der Filzstift	filts-shtift
female *adj.*	weiblich	vīp-likh
ferry	die Fähre	fairer
festival	das Fest	fest
fetch (to)	holen	hohlen
few	wenig	vaynikh
fiancé(e)	der/die Verlobte	fairlohbter
field	das Feld	felt
fight (to)	kämpfen	kaimpfen
fill (to)	füllen	fuillen
fill in (to)	ausfüllen	owsfuillen
film	der Film	film
find (to)	finden	feenden
fine	die Geldstrafe	gelt-shtrahfer
finish (to)	vollenden	follenden
finished	fertig	fairtikh
fire	das Feuer	foyer

fire escape	der Notausgang	noht-owsgang
fire extinguisher	der Feuerlöscher	foyair-lershair
fireworks *display*	das Feuerwerk	foyair-vairk
fireworks *individual*	die Feuerwerkskörper	foyairvairks-kerpair
first	erste	airster
first-aid	die erste Hilfe	airster heelfer
first class	die erste Klasse	airster klasser
fish	der Fisch	fish
fish (to)	angeln	angeln
fisherman	der Fischer	fisher
fishing tackle	die Angelgeräte	angell-gerayter
fit	fähig	fay-ikh
fit (to)	passen	passen
flag	die Fahne	fahner
flat *adj.*	flach	flakh
flat *noun*	die Wohnung	vohnoong
flavour *taste*	der Geschmack	geshmak
flavour *flavouring*	das Aroma	ahrohmah
flea market	der Flohmarkt	flohmarkt
flight	der Flug	floog
flippers	die Schwimmflossen	shvimflossen
float (to)	obenauf schwimmen	ohbenowf shvimmen
flood	die Flut	floot
floor	der Fussboden	foos-bohden
floor *storey*	der Stock	shtock

floor show	**das Kabarett**	kabarett
flower	**die Blume**	bloomer
fly	**die Fliege**	fleeger
fly (to)	**fliegen**	fleegen
fog	**der Nebel**	naybel
fold (to)	**falten**	falten
follow (to)	**folgen**	folgen
food	**das Essen**	essen
foot	**der Fuss**	foos
football	**der Fussball**	foos-bal
footpath	**der Fussweg**	foos-vayg
for	**für**	fuir
forbid (to)	**verbieten**	fairbeeten
foreign	**fremd**	fremt
forest	**der Wald**	valt
forget (to)	**vergessen**	fairgessen
fork	**die Gabel**	gahbel
forward	**vorwärts**	fohrvairts
forward (to)	**nachschicken**	nahkhshicken
fountain	**der (Spring)brunnen**	(shpring)broonen
fragile	**zerbrechlich**	tsairbrekhlikh
free	**frei**	frī
freight	**die Fracht**	frakht
fresh	**frisch**	frish
fresh water	**das Süsswasser**	zuis-vassair

friend	der Freund/die Freundin	froynt/froyndin
friendly	freundlich	froyntlikh
from	von	fon
front	die Vorderseite	forderzīter
frontier	die Grenze	grentser
frost	der Frost	frost
frozen *food*	tiefgekühlt/gefroren	teefgekuihlt/gefrohren
fruit	die Frucht	frookht
full	voll	foll
fun	der Spass	shpahs
funny	komisch	kohmish
fur	der Pelz	pelts
furniture	die Möbel, der Hausrat	merbel, howsraht

G

gallery	die Galerie	gallairee
gamble (to)	(um Geld) spielen	(oom gelt) shpeelen
game	das Spiel	shpeel
garage	die Garage	garahjer
garbage	der Abfall	apfal
garden	der Garten	garten
gas	das Gas	gas
gate	das Tor	tohr
gentleman	der Herr/Mann	hair/man

genuine	**echt**	ekht
German *adj.*	**deutsch**	doytsh
German *noun*	**der Deutsche**	doytsher
Germany	**Deutschland**	doytshlant
get (to)	**bekommen**	bekommen
get off (to)	**aussteigen**	ows-shtīgen
get on (to)	**einsteigen**	īn-shtīgen
gift	**das Geschenk**	geshenk
gift wrap (to)	**in Geschenkpapier einwickeln**	in geshenkpahpeer īnvikeln
girdle	**der Hüftgürtel**	huift-guirtell
girl	**das Mädchen**	mayd-khen
give (to)	**geben**	gayben
glad	**froh**	froh
glass	**das Glas**	glahs
glasses	**die Brille**	briller
gloomy	**dunkel/schwermütig**	doonkell/shvairmuitikh
glorious	**herrlich**	hairlikh
glove	**der Handschuh**	hant-shoo
go (to)	**gehen**	gayen
goal	**das Ziel**	tseel
goal (to score a)	**ein Tor schiessen**	tohr sheessen
god	**der Gott**	got
gold	**das Gold**	golt
gold plate	**die Vergoldung**	fairgoldoong
golf course	**der Golfplatz**	golfplats

good	**gut**	goot
government	**die Regierung**	regeeroong
granddaughter	**die Enkelin**	enkellin
grandfather	**der Grossvater**	grohs-fahtair
grandmother	**die Grossmutter**	grohs-moottair
grandson	**der Enkel**	enkel
grass	**das Gras**	grahs
grateful	**dankbar**	dankbahr
gravel	**der Kies**	kees
great	**gross**	grohs
groceries	**die Lebensmittel**	laybensmittel
ground	**der Grund/der Boden**	groont/bohden
grow (to)	**wachsen**	vaksen
guarantee	**die Garantie**	garantee
guard	**der Schaffner**	shaffnair
guest	**der Gast**	gast
guest house	**das Gästehaus**	gesterhows
guide, guide book	**der Führer**	fuirer
guided tour	**die Führung**	fuiroong

H

hail	**der Hagel**	hahgel
hair	**das Haar**	hahr
hair brush	**die Haarbürste**	hahr-buirster
hair dryer	**der Föhn**	fern

hairgrip	**die Haarklammer**	hahrklammer
hairpin	**die Haarnadel**	hahrnahdel
hair spray	**der Haarspray**	hahrspray
half	**halb**	halp
half fare	**der halbe Preis**	halber prīs
hammer	**der Hammer**	hammer
hand	**die Hand**	hant
handbag	**die Handtasche**	hant-tasher
handkerchief	**das Taschentuch**	tashentookh
handmade	**handgearbeitet**	hantgayarbītet
hang (to)	**hängen**	hengen
happen (to)	**geschehen**	geshayen
happy	**glücklich**	gluiklikh
happy birthday	**herzlichen Glückwunsch zum Geburtstag**	hairtsleekhen gluikvoonsh tsoom geboortstahg
harbour	**der Hafen**	hahfen
hard	**hart**	hart
hard *difficult*	**schwierig**	shveerikh
hardly	**kaum**	kowm
harmful	**schädlich**	shaytleekh
harmless	**harmlos**	harmlohs
hat	**der Hut**	hoot
have (to)	**haben**	hahben
haversack	**der Rucksack**	rookzak
he	**er**	air
headphones	**die Kopfhörer**	kopfherair

health	die Gesundheit	gezoont-hīt
hear (to)	hören	her-ren
heart	das Herz	hairts
heat	die Hitze	hitser
heating	die Heizung	hītsoong
heavy	schwer	shvair
hedge	die Hecke	hecker
heel *shoe*	der Absatz	apzats
height	die Höhe	her-her
helicopter	der Hubschrauber	hoob-shrowbair
help	die Hilfe	heelfer
help (to)	helfen	helfen
hem	der Saum	zowm
her	sie/ihr/ihre	zee/eer/eerer
here	hier	heer
hers	ihr	eer
high	hoch	hohkh
hike (to)	wandern	vandairn
hill	der Hügel/Berg	huigel/bairg
him	ihn/ihm	een/eem
hire (to)	mieten	meeten
his	sein/seine	zīn/zīner
history	die Geschichte	geshikhter
hitch hike (to)	per Anhalter fahren	pair anhaltair fahren
hobby	das Hobby	hobbee
hold (to)	(fest)halten	(fest)halten

hole	**das Loch**	lokh
holiday	**der Feiertag**	fiyairtahg
holidays	**die Ferien**	fayree-en
hollow	**hohl**	hohl
(at) home	**zu Hause**	tsoo howzer
honeymoon	**die Hochzeitsreise**	hokh-tsīts-rīzer
hope	**die Hoffnung**	hofnoong
hope (to)	**hoffen**	hoffen
horse	**das Pferd**	pfayrt
horse races	**das Pferderennen**	pfayrder-rennen
horse riding	**das (Pferde)reiten**	(pfayrde)rīten
hose	**der Schlauch**	shlowkh
hospital	**das Krankenhaus**	krankenhows
host	**der Gastgeber**	gastgayber
hostel	**die Herberge**	hairbairger
hostess	**die Gastgeberin**	gastgayberin
hot	**heiss**	hīs
hotel	**das Hotel**	hohtel
hotel keeper	**der Hotelier**	hohtel-yay
hot water bottle	**die Wärmflasche**	vairmflasher
hour	**die Stunde**	shtoonder
house	**das Haus**	hows
hovercraft	**das Hovercraft**	hovairkrahft
how?	**wie?**	vee
how much, many?	**wie viel/wie viele?**	vee feel/vee feeler
hungry	**hungrig**	hoongrikh

hunt (to)	**jagen**	yahgen
hurry (to)	**eilen**	īlen
hurt (to)	**schmerzen/weh tun**	shmairtsen/vay toon
husband	**der Mann/Gatte**	man/gatter
hydrofoil	**das Tragflächenboot**	trahgflekhenboht

I

I	**ich**	ikh
ice	**das Eis**	īs
ice cream	**das Eis**	īs
ice lolly	**das Eis am Stiel**	īs am shteel
identify (to)	**identifizieren**	eedenteefeezeeren
if	**wenn**	ven
imagine (to)	**(sich) vorstellen**	fohrshtellen (zeekh)
immediately	**sofort**	sohfort
important	**wichtig**	vikhtikh
in	**in**	in
include (to)	**einschliessen**	īn-shleessen
included	**einbegriffen**	īn-begriffen
inconvenient	**ungelegen**	oongelaygen
incorrect	**unrichtig/falsch**	oonreekhtikh/falsh
indeed	**tatsächlich**	tahtsekhlikh
independent	**unabhängig**	oonaphengeekh
indoors	**drinnen**	drinnen
industry	**die Industrie**	indoostree
inexpensive	**preiswert**	prīsvairt

inflammable	**feuergefährlich**	foyairgefayrleekh
inflatable	**aufblasbar**	owfblahsbahr
inflation	**die Inflation**	inflahtsyohn
information	**die Auskunft**	owskoonft
information bureau	**die Auskunftsstelle**	owskoonfts-shteller
ink	**die Tinte**	tinter
inn	**das Gasthaus**	gasthows
insect	**das Insekt**	inzekt
insect bite	**der Insektenstich**	inzekten-shtikh
insect repellant	**das Insektenbe-kämpfungsmittel**	inzekten-bekempfoongs-mittel
inside	**drinnen**	drinnen
instead of	**statt**	shtat
instructor	**der Lehrer**	layrer
insurance	**die Versicherung**	fair-zikhairoong
insure (to)	**versichern**	fair-zikhairn
insured	**versichert**	fairzeekhairt
interest	**das Interesse**	intairesser
interested	**interessiert**	intairesseert
interesting	**interessant**	intairessant
interpreter	**der Dolmetscher**	dolmetsher
into	**in**	in
introduce (to)	**bekanntmachen**	bekant-makhen
invitation	**die Einladung**	īn-lahdoong
invite (to)	**einladen**	īn-lahden
Ireland	**Irland**	eer-lant

Irish	**irisch**	eerish
iron (to)	**bügeln, plätten**	buigeln, pletten
island	**die Insel**	eenzell
it	**es**	es

J

jacket	**die Jacke**	yacker
jar	**der Krug/Topf**	kroog/topf
jelly fish	**die Qualle**	k-valler
Jew	**der Jude**	yooder
jewellery	**der Schmuck**	shmoock
Jewish	**jüdisch**	yuidish
job	**die Stellung**	shtelloong
journey	**die Reise**	rīzer
jump (to)	**springen**	shpringen
jumper	**der Pullover**	poolohvair

K

keep (to)	**halten/behalten**	halten/behalten
key	**der Schlüssel**	shluissel
kick (to)	**(mit dem Fuss) stossen**	mit dem foos shtohsen
kind *friendly*	**freundlich**	froyntlikh
king	**der König**	kernikh
kiss	**der Kuss**	koos
kiss (to)	**küssen**	kuissen

kitchen	**die Küche**	kuikher
knickers	**der Schlüpfer**	shluipfair
knife	**das Messer**	messair
knock (to)	**klopfen**	klopfen
know (to) *fact*	**wissen**	vissen
know (to) *person*	**kennen**	kennen

L

label	**das Etikett**	eteekett
lace	**die Spitze**	shpitser
lady	**die Dame/Frau**	dahmer/frow
lake	**der See**	zay
lamp	**die Lampe**	lamper
land	**das Land**	lant
landing	**die Landung**	landoong
landlady/lord	**die Hauswirtin/der Hauswirt**	howsveertin/howsveert
landmark	**das Kennzeichen**	kenn-tsīkhen
landscape	**die Landschaft**	lantshaft
lane *town*	**die Gasse**	gasser
lane *country*	**der Pfad**	pfaht
language	**die Sprache**	shprahkher
large	**gross**	grohs
last	**letzt**	letst
late	**spät**	shpayt
laugh (to)	**lachen**	lakhen

laundrette	die Münzwäscherei	muints-veshairī
lavatory	die Toilette	twaletter
lavatory paper	das Toilettenpapier	twaletten-papeer
law	das Gesetz	gezets
lawn	der Rasen	rahzen
lawyer	der Rechtsanwalt	rekhts-anvalt
lead (to)	führen	fuiren
leaf	das Blatt	blat
leak (to)	auslaufen	owslowfen
learn (to)	lernen	lairnen
least	mindest/wenigst	mindest/vaynikhst
(in the) least	am wenigsten	am vaynikhsten
leather	das Leder	layder
leave (to) *abandon*	verlassen	fairlassen
leave (to) *go away*	abfahren	apfahren
(on the) left	links	leenks
left luggage	die Gepäckaufbewahrung	gepeck-owf-bevahroong
lend (to)	leihen	lī-en
length	die Länge	lenger
less	weniger	vaynigair
lesson	der Unterricht	oonter-rikht
let (to) *rent*	vermieten	fairmeeten
let (to) *allow*	erlauben/lassen	airlowben/lassen
letter	der Brief	breef
level crossing	der Bahnübergang	bahnuibergang

library	**die Bibliothek**	beeblee-ohtayk
licence	**die Erlaubnis**	airlowbnis
life	**das Leben**	layben
lifebelt	**der Rettungsgürtel**	rettoongs-guirtel
lifeboat	**das (Lebens)rettungsboot**	(laybens)rettoongs-boht
lifeguard	**der Rettungsschwimmer**	rettoongs-shvimmair
lift	**der Fahrstuhl**	fahr-shtool
light *colour*	**hell**	hell
light *weight*	**leicht**	līkht
light *noun*	**das Licht**	likht
lighter	**das Feuerzeug**	foyair-tsoyg
lighter fuel	**das Feuerzeugbenzin**	foyairtsoyg-bentseen
lighthouse	**der Leuchtturm**	loykht-toorm
lightning	**der Blitz**	blits
like (to)	**gern haben**	gairn hahben
line	**die Linie**	leenee-yer
linen *fibre*	**das Leinen**	līnen
linen *household*	**die Bettwäsche**	betvesher
lingerie	**die Unterwäsche**	oontervesher
lipsalve	**der Lippenbalsam**	lippenbalzahm
lipstick	**der Lippenstift**	lippen-shtift
liquid *adj.*	**flüssig**	fluisseekh
liquid *noun*	**die Flüssigkeit**	fluisseekh-kīt
listen (to)	**zuhören**	tsooher-ren

little	**klein**	klīn
live (to)	**leben**	layben
loaf	**das Brot**	broht
local	**lokal/hiesig/örtlich**	lohkahl/heeseekh/ertlikh
lock	**das Schloss**	shloss
lock (to)	**schliessen**	shleessen
long	**lang**	lang
look at (to)	**ansehen**	anzayen
look for (to)	**suchen**	zookhen
look like (to)	**aussehen**	ows-zayen
loose	**los(e)**	lohs (lohzer)
lorry	**der Lastwagen**	lastvahgen
lose (to)	**verlieren**	fairleeren
lost property office	**das Fundbüro**	foont-buiroh
(a) lot	**(sehr) viel**	(zayr) feel
loud	**laut**	lowt
love (to)	**lieben**	leeben
lovely	**schön**	shern
low	**niedrig**	needrikh
lucky	**Glücks..., glücklich**	gluiks..., gluikleekh
lucky (to be)	**Glück haben**	gluik hahben
luggage	**das Gepäck**	gepeck
(piece of) luggage	**das Gepäckstück**	gepeckshtuik
lunch	**das Mittagessen**	meetahgessen

M

mad	verrückt	fair-ruikt
magazine	die Zeitschrift	tsīt-shrift
maid	das (Dienst)mädchen	(deenst)maydkhen
mail	die Post	post
main street	die Hauptstrasse	howptstrahser
make (to)	machen	makhen
male *adj.*	männlich	menlikh
man	der Mann	man
manage (to)	auskommen	owskommen
manager	der Leiter	līter
manicure	die Maniküre	maneekuirer
man-made	künstlich	kuinst-leekh
many	viel(e)	feel(er)
map	die Karte	karter
market	der Markt	markt
married	verheiratet	fairhīrahtet
marsh	die Marsch	marsh
Mass	die Messe	messer
massage	die Massage	massahjer
match	das Streichholz	strīkh-holts
match *sport*	das Spiel	shpeel
material	der Stoff	shtof
matinée	die Matinee	mateenay
mattress	die Matratze	matrattser
me	mich/mir	meekh/meer

meal	die Mahlzeit	mahltsīt
mean (to)	bedeuten	bedoyten
measurements	die Masse	masser
meet (to)	treffen	treffen
mend (to)	reparieren	raypareeren
menstruation	die Periode/Regel	payreeohder/raygel
mess	die Unordnung	oonordnoong
message	die Nachricht	nahkh-rikht
messenger	der Bote	bohter
metal	das Metall	maytal
midday	der Mittag	mittakh
middle	die Mitte	mitter
middle aged	in mittlerem Alter	in mitlerem altair
middle class	die Mittelklasse	mittelklasser
midnight	die Mitternacht	mittair-nahkht
mild	mild	milt
mill	die Mühle	muiler
mine *pron.*	mein	mīn
minute	die Minute	meenooter
mirror	der Spiegel	shpeegel
Miss	Fräulein	froylīn
miss (to)	verpassen	fairpassen
mistake	der Fehler	faylair
mix (to)	(ver)mischen	(fair)mishen
mixed	gemischt	gemisht
modern	modern	mohdairn

moisturizer	**die Feuchtigkeits(creme)**	foykhteekh-kīts(-kraymer)
moment	**der Augenblick**	owgen-blick
monastery	**das Kloster**	klohstair
money	**das Geld**	gelt
monk	**der Mönch**	mernkh
month	**der Monat**	mohnaht
monument	**das Denkmal**	denkmahl
moon	**der Mond**	mohnt
moorland	**das Sumpfland**	zoompflant
moped	**das Moped**	mohpet
more	**mehr**	mayr
morning	**der Morgen**	morgen
mosque	**die Moschee**	moshay
most	**meist/die meisten**	mīst/mīsten
mother	**die Mutter**	moottair
motor bike	**das Motorrad**	motohr-raht
motor boat	**das Motorboot**	mohtor-boht
motor cycle	**das Motorrad**	mohtor-raht
motor racing	**das Autorennen**	owtoh-rennen
motorway	**die Autobahn**	owtohbahn
mountain	**der Berg**	bairg
mouse	**die Maus**	mows
mouthwash	**das Mundwasser**	moontvassair
move (to)	**bewegen**	bevaygen
Mr	**Herr**	hair

Mrs	Frau	frow
much	viel	feel
museum	das Museum	moozayoom
music	die Musik	moozeek
must *to have to*	müssen	muissen
my	mein/meine	mīn/mīner
myself	mich	mikh

N

nail	der Nagel	nahgel
nailbrush	die Nagelbürste	nahgel-buirster
nailfile	die Nagelfeile	nahgel-filer
nail polish	der Nagellack	nahgel-lak
name	der Name	nahmer
napkin	die Serviette	zairveeyetter
nappy	die Windel	vindel
narrow	schmal	shmahl
natural	natürlich	nahtuirleekh
near	in der Nähe von ...	in dair nayer fon ...
nearly	fast	fast
necessary	notwendig	nohtvendikh
necklace	die (Hals)kette	(hals)ketter
need (to)	brauchen	browkhen
needle	die Nadel	nahdel
nephew	der Neffe	neffer
net	das Netz	nets

never	**nie/niemals**	nee/neemals
new	**neu**	noy
news	**die Nachrichten**	nakh-rikhten
newspaper	**die Zeitung**	tsītoong
New Zealand	**Neuseeland**	noyzaylant
next	**nächst**	naikhst
nice	**nett**	net
niece	**die Nichte**	nikhter
night	**die Nacht**	nakht
nightclub	**der Nachtklub**	nakht-kloob
nightdress	**das Nachthemd**	nakht-hemt
nobody	**niemand**	neemant
noisy	**lärmend**	lairment
non-alcoholic	**nicht-alkoholisch**	nikht-alkoh-**hohleesh**
none	**keine/keinen**	kīner/kīnen
no one	**niemand**	neemant
normal	**normal**	normahl
north	**der Norden**	norden
nosebleed	**das Nasenbluten**	nahzen-blooten
not	**nicht**	nikht
(bank) note	**der Geldschein**	geltshīn
notebook	**das Notizbuch**	nohteets-bookh
nothing	**nichts**	nikhts
notice	**die Notiz**	nohteets
notice (to)	**bemerken**	bemairken
novel	**der Roman**	rohmahn

now	jetzt	yetst
number	die Nummer/Zahl	noommair/tsahl
nylon	das Nylon	nīlon
nylons	die Nylonstrümpfe	nīlon-shtruimpfer

O

obtain (to)	erhalten	airhalten
occasion	die Gelegenheit	gelaygenhīt
occupation	die Beschäftigung	besheftigoong
occupied	besetzt	bezetst
ocean	das Meer	mayr
odd *not even*	ungerade	oongerahder
odd *strange*	sonderbar	zondairbahr
of	von	fon
of course	natürlich	nahtuirlikh
off	ab	ap
offer	das Angebot	angeboht
offer (to)	anbieten	anbeeten
office	das Büro	buiroh
officer, official	der Beamte	be-amter
officer *milit.*	der Offizier	offitseer
official *adj.*	offiziell	offitsyel
often	oft	oft
oily	fettig	fettikh
ointment	die Salbe	zalber
OK	in Ordnung/OK	in ohrdnoong/oh-kay

old	**alt**	alt
on	**auf/an**	owf/an
once	**einmal**	īn-mahl
on foot	**zu Fuss**	tsoo foos
only	**nur**	noor
on time	**rechtzeitig**	rekht-tsītikh
open (to)	**öffnen**	erfnen
open *p.p.*	**geöffnet**	ge-erfnet
open-air ...	**Freilicht ...**	frīlikht ...
opening	**die Öffnung**	erfnoong
opera	**die Oper**	ohpair
opportunity	**die Gelegenheit**	gelaygen-hīt
opposite	**gegenüber**	gaygen-uiber
optician	**der Optiker**	opteekair
or	**oder**	ohdair
orchard	**der Obstgarten**	ohpst-garten
orchestra	**das Orchester**	orkestair
order (to)	**bestellen**	beshtellen
ordinary	**gewöhnlich**	gevernlikh
other	**ander**	ander
otherwise	**sonst**	zonst
ought	**sollen**	zollen
our/ours	**unser**	oonzer
out	**aus**	ows
out of order	**ausser Betrieb**	owsair betreep
out of stock	**nicht vorrätig**	nikht fohr-rayteekh

outside	**draussen**	drowsen
over	**über**	uiber
over *finished*	**fertig/zu Ende**	fairtikh/tsoo ender
over there	**da drüben**	dah druiben
overcoat	**der Mantel**	mantel
overnight	**über Nacht**	uiber nakht
owe (to)	**schulden**	shoolden
owner	**der Besitzer**	bezit-tser

P

pack (to)	**packen**	packen
packet	**das Paket**	packayt
paddle *noun*	**das Paddel**	paddel
paddle (to)	**planschen**	planshen
paddling pool	**das Planschbecken**	plansh-becken
page	**die Seite**	zīter
paid	**bezahlt**	betsahlt
pain	**der Schmerz**	shmairts
paint (to)	**malen**	mahlen
painting	**das Gemälde**	gemaylder
pair	**das Paar**	pahr
palace	**der Palast**	palast
pale	**blass**	blas
paper	**das Papier**	papeer
parcel	**das Paket**	packayt
park	**der Park**	park

park (to)	**parken**	parken
parking disc	**die Parkscheibe**	parkshïber
parking meter	**der Parkautomat**	park-owtohmaht
parking ticket	**der Strafzettel**	shtrahf-tsettel
parliament	**das Parlament**	pahrlahment
part	**der Teil**	tïl
party	**die Gesellschaft**	gezel-shaft
pass (to)	**vorbeigehen**	forbï-gayen
passenger	**der Passagier**	passajeer
passport	**der Pass**	pass
past	**vorig/früher**	forikh/frui-air
path	**der Pfad**	pfaht
patient	**der Patient**	patsyent
pavement	**der Fusssteig**	foos-shtïg
pay (to)	**bezahlen**	betsahlen
payment	**die Zahlung**	tsahloong
peace	**der Friede**	freeder
peak	**der Gipfel**	geepfel
pearl	**die Perle**	pairler
pebble	**der Kiesel**	keezel
pedal	**das Pedal**	pedahl
pedestrian	**der Fussgänger**	foosgenger
pedestrian crossing	**der Fussgängerübergang**	foos-gengair-uibairgang
pedestrian precinct	**die Fussgängerzone**	foosgengair-tsohner
pen	**die Feder**	fayder

pencil	der Bleistift	blīshtift
penknife	das Taschenmesser	tashen-messair
pensioner	der Rentner	rentnair
people	die Leute	loyter
perfect	tadellos	tahdel-lohs
per (person)	pro (Person)	proh (pairzohn)
performance	die Aufführung	owf-fuiroong
perfume	das Parfüm	parfuim
perhaps	vielleicht	feelīkht
perishable	leicht verderblich	līkht fairdairblikh
permit	die Erlaubnis	airlowbnis
permit (to)	erlauben	airlowben
person	die Person	pairzohn
personal	persönlich	pairzernlikh
petrol	das Benzin	bentseen
petrol station	die Tankstelle	tank-shteller
petticoat	der Unterrock	oonter-rock
photograph	die Photographie	fohtoh-grafee
photographer	der Photograph	fohtoh-grahf
piano	das Klavier	klaveer
pick (to)	aussuchen	ows-zookhen
pick (to) *flowers*	pflücken	pfluiken
picnic	das Picknick	pick-nick
piece	das Stück	shtuik
pier	die Landungsbrücke	landoongs-bruiker
pillow	das Kopfkissen	kopf-kissen

pin	die Stecknadel	shteck-nahdel
(safety) pin	die Sicherheitsnadel	zeekhairhīts-nahdel
pipe	die Pfeife	pfīfer
place	der Ort	ort
plain	einfach	īn-fakh
plan	der Plan	plahn
plant	die Pflanze	pflantser
plastic	die Plastik	plasteek
plate	der Teller	tellair
platform	der Bahnsteig	bahn-shtīg
play	das Schauspiel	show-shpeel
play (to)	spielen	shpeelen
player	der Spieler	shpeelair
please	bitte	bitter
pleased	froh	froh
plenty	die Menge	menger
pliers	die Zange *sing.*	tsanger
plimsoll	der Turnschuh	toorn-shoo
plug	der Stöpsel	shterpsel
plug *electric*	der Stecker	shteckair
pocket	die Tasche	tasher
point	der Punkt	poonkt
poisonous	giftig	giftikh
policeman	der Polizist	pohleetsist
police station	die Polizeiwache	pohleetsī-vakher
political	politisch	pohleetish

politician	der Politiker	pohleeteekair
politics	die Politik	pohleeteek
pollution	die Verschmutzung	fairshmootsoong
pond	der Teich	tīkh
poor	arm	arm
pope	der Papst	pahpst
popular	populär	pohpoolair
porcelain	das Porzellan	portsellahn
port	der Hafen	hahfen
possible	möglich	merglikh
post (to)	einstecken/aufgeben	īn-shtecken/owf-gayben
post box	der Briefkasten	breef-kasten
postcard	die Postkarte	post-karter
postman	der Briefträger	breef-trayger
post office	die Post	post
postpone (to)	zurückstellen	tsooruikshtellen
pound	das Pfund	pfoont
powder	der Puder	poodair
prefer (to)	vorziehen	fohrtseeyen
pregnant	schwanger	shvangair
prepare (to)	vorbereiten	fohrberīten
present *gift*	das Geschenk	geshaink
president	der President	prayzeedent
press (to)	bügeln/plätten	buigeln/pletten
pretty	hübsch	huipsh
price	der Preis	prīs

priest	der Priester	preestair
prime minister	der Premierminister	premyay-ministair
print	der (Ab)druck	(ap)droock
print (to)	abdrucken	(ap)droocken
private	privat/persönlich	preevaht/pairzernlikh
problem	das Problem	problaym
profession	der Beruf	beroof
programme	das Programm	prohgram
promise	das Versprechen	fairshprekhen
promise (to)	versprechen	fairshprekhen
prompt	sofortig	zohfortikh
protestant	der Protestant	prohtestant
provide (to)	besorgen	bezorgen
public	öffentlich	erfentlikh
public holiday	der öffentliche Feiertag	erfentleekher fiair-tahg
pull (to)	ziehen	tseeyen
pump	die Pumpe	poomper
pure	rein	rīn
purse	das Portemonnaie	portmonnay
push (to)	stossen	shtohssen
put (to)	stellen	shtellen
pyjamas	der Schlafanzug	shlahf-antsoog

Q

quality	die Qualität	kvaleetayt

quantity	**die Quantität**	kvanteetayt
quarter	**das Viertel**	feertel
queen	**die Königin**	kerneegin
question	**die Frage**	frahger
queue	**die Schlange**	shlanger
queue (to)	**Schlange stehen**	shlanger shtayen
quick(ly)	**schnell**	shnel
quiet(ly)	**ruhig**	roo-ikh
quite	**ganz**	gants

R

race	**das Rennen**	rennen
racecourse	**die Rennbahn**	rennbahn
radiator	**der Heizkörper**	hīts-kerper
radio	**das Radio**	rahdeeyoh
railway	**die Eisenbahn**	īzen-bahn
rain	**der Regen**	raygen
rain (to)	**regnen**	raygnen
raincoat	**der Regenmantel**	raygen-mantel
rare	**selten**	zelten
rash	**der Ausschlag**	ows-shlahg
rate	**die Gebühr**	gebuihr
rather	**ziemlich**	tseemlikh
raw	**roh**	roh
razor	**der Rasierapparat**	razeer-aparaht
razor blade	**die Rasierklinge**	razeer-klinger

reach (to)	**reichen**	rīkhen
read (to)	**lesen**	layzen
ready	**bereit**	berīt
real	**wahr**	vahr
really	**wirklich**	veerklikh
reason	**der Grund**	groont
receipt	**die Quittung**	k-veetoong
receive (to)	**bekommen**	bekommen
recent	**neu**	noy
recipe	**das Rezept**	raytsept
recognize (to)	**erkennen**	airkennen
recommend (to)	**empfehlen**	empfaylen
record	**die Schallplatte**	shalplatter
record *sport*	**der Rekord**	record
refill	**Nachfüll ...**	nahkhfuil ...
refill (to)	**nachfüllen**	nahkhfuillen
refreshments	**die Erfrischungen**	airfrishoongen
refrigerator	**der Kühlschrank**	kuilshrank
refund	**die Rückzahlung**	ruiktsahloong
regards	**die Grüsse**	gruisser
register (to)	**(Gepäck) aufgeben/ einschreiben**	(gepeck) owfgayben/īn- shrīben
relative	**der Verwandter/die Verwandte**	fairvandtair/fairvandter
religion	**die Religion**	rayligyohn
remember (to)	**sich erinnern**	zikh airinnairn
rent	**die Miete**	meeter

rent (to)	mieten/leihen	meeten/lī-en
repair (to)	reparieren	repahreer'en
repeat (to)	wiederholen	veederhohlen
reply (to)	antworten	antvorten
reservation	die Reservierung	rezairveeroong
reserve (to)	reservieren	rezairveeren
reserved	reserviert	rayzairveert
restaurant	das Restaurant	restorant
restaurant car	der Speisewagen	shpīzer-vahgen
return (to)	zurückkehren	tsooruik-kairen
return (to) *give back*	zurückgeben	tsooruik-gayben
reward	die Belohnung	belohnoong
ribbon	das Band	bant
rich	reich	rīkh
ride	die Fahrt	fahrt
ride (to)	reiten	rīten
right *opp. left*	rechts	rekhts
right *opp. wrong*	richtig	rikhtikh
ring	der Ring	ring
ripe	reif	rīf
rise (to)	sich erheben	zikh airhayben
rise (to) *get up*	aufstehen	owfshtayen
river	der Fluss	floos
road	die Strasse	shtrahsser
road map	die Strassenkarte	shtrahssen-karter
road sign	das Vehrkehrsschild	fairkayrs-shilt

road works	**die Bauarbeiten**	bowarbīten
rock	**der Felsen**	felzen
roll (to)	**rollen**	rollen
roof	**das Dach**	dakh
room	**das Zimmer**	tsimmair
rope	**das Seil**	zīl
rotten	**faul**	fowl
rough	**rauh/grob**	row/grohp
round	**rund**	roont
rowing boat	**das Ruderboot**	rooder-boht
rubber	**das Gummi**	goomee
rubbish	**der Abfall**	apfal
rucksack	**der Rucksack**	rookzak
rude	**unverschämt**	oonfairshaymt
ruin	**die Ruine**	roo-eener
ruins	**die Ruine**	roo-eener
rule (to)	**beherrschen**	behairshen
run (to)	**laufen**	lowfen

S

sad	**traurig**	trowrikh
saddle	**der Sattel**	zattel
safe	**sicher**	zeekhair
sail	**das Segel**	zaygel
sailing boat	**das Segelboot**	zaygel-boht

sailor(s)	der Seeman (die Seeleute)	zayman (zayloyter)
sale *clearance*	der Ausverkauf	owsfairkowf
(for) sale	verkäuflich	fairkoyflikh
saleswoman	die Verkäuferin	fairkoyferin
salesman	der Verkäufer	fairkoyfair
salt water	das Salzwasser	zalts-vassair
same	der-/die-/dasselbe	zelber
sand	der Sand	zant
sandal	die Sandale	zandahler
sanitary towel	die Binde	binder
satisfactory	befriedigend	befreedigent
saucer	die Untertasse	oontertasser
save (to)	retten	retten
say (to)	sagen	zahgen
scald (to)	verbrühen	fairbruien
scarf	der Schal	shahl
scenery	die Landschaft	lantshaft
scent	das Parfüm	parfuim
school	die Schule	shooler
scissors	die Schere	shairer
Scotland	Schottland	shotlant
Scottish	schottisch	shottish
scratch (to)	kratzen	kratsen
screw	die Schraube	shrowber
screwdriver	der Schraubenzieher	shrowbentsee-er

sculpture	**die Skulptur**	skoolptoor
sea	**das Meer/die See**	mayr/zay
sea food	**die Meeresfrüchte**	mayres-fruikhter
seasickness	**die Seekrankheit**	zay-krank-hīt
season	**die Jahreszeit**	yahres-tsīt
seat	**der Platz**	plats
seat belt	**der Sicherheitsgurt**	zeekher-hītsgoort
second	**zweite**	tsvīter
second hand	**gebraucht**	gebrowkht
see (to)	**sehen**	zayen
seem (to)	**scheinen**	shīnen
self-catering service	**die Selbstbedienung**	zelpst-bedeenoong
self-contained *e.g. of flat*	**separat**	zaypahraht
sell (to)	**verkaufen**	fairkowfen
send (to)	**schicken**	shicken
separate	**getrennt**	getrent
serious	**ernst**	airnst
serve (to)	**bedienen**	bedeenen
served	**serviert**	zairveert
service	**die Bedienung**	bedeenoong
service *church*	**der Gottesdienst**	gottesdeenst
several	**mehrere**	mayrerer
sew (to)	**nähen**	nayen
shade *colour*	**der Farbton**	farptohn
shade/shadow	**der Schatten**	shatten

shallow	**flach**	flakh
shampoo	**das Schampoo**	shampoo
shape	**die Form**	form
share (to)	**teilen**	tīlen
sharp	**scharf**	sharf
shave (to)	**rasieren**	rahzeeren
shaving brush	**der Rasierpinsel**	rahzeer-pinzel
shaving cream	**die Rasiercreme**	rahzeer-kraymer
she	**sie**	zee
sheet	**das Bettlaken**	betlahken
shelf	**das Regal**	raygahl
shell	**die Muschel**	mooshell
shelter	**das Obdach**	opdakh
shine (to)	**scheinen**	shīnen
shingle	**der Kiesel**	keezel
ship	**das Schiff**	shiff
shipping line	**die Schifffahrts-gesellschaft**	shiff-fahrts-gezellshaft
shirt	**das Hemd**	hemt
shock	**der Stoss/Schock**	shtohs/shock
shoe	**der Schuh**	shoo
shoelace	**der Schnürsenkel**	shnuir-zenkel
shoe polish	**die Schuhcreme**	shookraymer
shop	**der Laden/das Geschäft**	lahden/gesheft
shopping centre	**das Einkaufszentrum**	īn-kowfs-tsentroom
shore	**das Ufer/die Küste**	oofair/kuister

short	**kurz**	koorts
shorts	**die Shorts**	shorts
show	**die Vorstellung**	fohrshtelloong
show (to)	**zeigen**	tsīgen
shower	**die Dusche**	doosher
shut (to)	**schliessen**	shleessen
shut *p.p.*	**geschlossen**	geshlossen
side	**die Seite**	zīter
sights	**die Sehenswürdig-keiten**	sayens-vuirdikh-kīten
sightseeing	**die Besichtigung von Sehenswürdig-keiten**	bezikhtigoong von zayens-vuirdikh-kīten
sign	**das Zeichen**	tsīkhen
sign *road*	**das (Strassen)schild**	(shtrahsen)shilt
sign (to)	**unterschreiben**	oontair-shrīben
signpost	**der Wegweiser**	vayk-vīzer
silver	**das Silber**	zilbair
simple	**einfach**	īnfakh
since	**seit**	zīt
sing (to)	**singen**	zingen
single	**einzig/einzeln**	īntsig/īntseln
single room	**das Einzelzimmer**	īntsel-tsimmer
sister	**die Schwester**	shvester
sit (to)	**sitzen**	zitsen
sit down (to)	**sich setzen**	zikh zetsen
size	**die Grösse**	grerser

skating	das Schlittschuh-laufen	shlitshoo-lowfen
skid (to)	rutschen	rootshen
skiing	das Skilaufen	shee-lowfen
skirt	der Rock	rock
sky	der Himmel	himmel
sleep (to)	schlafen	shlahfen
sleeper	der Schlafwagen	shlahf-vahgen
sleeping bag	der Schlafsack	shlahf-zack
sleeve	der Ärmel	airmel
slice	die Schnitte	shnitter
slip	der Unterrock	oonter-rock
slipper	der Hausschuh	hows-shoo
slowly	langsam	langzam
small	klein	klīn
smart	schick	shick
smell	der Geruch	gerookh
smell (to)	riechen	reekhen
smile (to)	lächeln	lekheln
smoke (to)	rauchen	rowkhen
(no) smoking	rauchen (verboten)	rowkhen (fairbohten)
smoking compartment	Raucher	rowkhair
non-smoking compartment	Nicht-Raucher	neekht-rowkhair
snack	der Imbiss	imbiss
snow	der Schnee	shnay
snow (to)	schneien	shnī-yen

so	**so**	zoh
soap	**die Seife**	zīfer
soap powder	**das Seifenpulver**	zīfenpoolvair
sober	**nüchtern**	nuikhtairn
sock	**die Socke**	zocker
soft	**weich**	vīkh
sold	**verkauft**	fairkowft
sold out	**ausverkauft**	owsfairkowft
sole *shoe*	**die Sohle**	zohler
solid	**fest**	fest
some	**einige/etwas**	īneeger/etvas
somebody	**jemand**	yaymant
somehow	**irgendwie**	eergentvee
something	**etwas**	etvas
sometimes	**manchmal**	mankhmahl
somewhere	**irgendwo**	eergentvoh
son	**der Sohn**	zohn
song	**das Lied**	leet
soon	**bald**	balt
sort	**die Art**	ahrt
sound	**der Laut**	lowt
sour	**sauer**	zower
south	**der Süden**	zuiden
souvenir	**das Andenken**	andenken
space	**der Raum**	rowm

spanner	der Schrauben-schlüssel	shrowben-shluissel
spare	Ersatz-/Reserve-	airzats/rezairver
speak (to)	sprechen	shprekhen
speciality	die Spezialität	shpaytseeyalitayt
spectacles	die Brille *sing.*	briller
speed	die Geschwindigkeit	geshvindikh-kīt
speed limit	die Geschwindigkeits-grenze	geshvindikhkīts-grentser
spend (to)	ausgeben	owsgayben
spice	das Gewürz	gevuirtz
spoon	der Löffel	lerffel
sport	der Sport	shport
sprain (to)	verstauchen	fairshtowkhen
spring	der Frühling/das Frühjahr	fruiling/fruiyahr
spring *water*	die Quelle	kveller
square	viereckig	feer-ekikh
square *noun*	der Platz	plats
square meter	das Quadratmeter	kvadrahtmaytair
stable	der Stall	shtal
stage	die Bühne	buiner
stain	der Fleck	fleck
stained	beschmutzt	beshmootst
stairs	die Treppe	trepper
stale	schal	shahl

stalls	**der Sperrsitz**	**shpair**-zits
stamp	**die Briefmarke**	breefmarker
stand (to)	**stehen**	**shtayen**
star	**der Stern**	shtairn
start (to)	**anfangen**	anfangen
(main) station	**der (Haupt)bahnhof**	(howpt)bahnhohf
statue	**die Statue**	shtah-too-er
stay (to)	**bleiben**	blīben
step	**der Schritt**	shrit
steward	**der Steward**	shtoo-art
stewardess	**die Stewardess**	shtoo-ardess
stick	**der Stock**	shtock
stiff	**starr**	shtar
still *not moving*	**still**	shtil
still *time*	**noch**	nokh
sting	**der Stich**	steekh
stocking	**der Strumpf**	shtroompf
stolen	**gestohlen**	geshtohlen
stone	**der Stein**	shtīn
stool	**der Stuhl/Hocker**	shtool/hockair
stop (to)	**(an)halten**	(an)halten
storm	**der Sturm**	shtoorm
stove	**der Ofen**	ohfen
straight	**gerade**	gerahder
straight on	**geradeaus**	gerahder-ows
strange	**sonderbar**	zondairbahr

strap	der Riemen	reemen
stream	der Bach	bakh
street	die Strasse	strahsser
stretch (to)	(aus)strecken	(ows)shtrecken
string	die Schnur	shnoor
strong	stark	shtark
student	der Student/die Studentin	shtoodent/shtoodentin
stung (to be)	gestochen werden	geshtokhen vairden
style	der Stil	shteel
suburb	der Vorort	fohrort
subway	die Unterführung	oonterfuiroong
such	solch	solkh
suddenly	plötzlich	plertsleekh
suede	das Wildleder	vilt-laydair
sugar	der Zucker	tsoocker
suggestion	der Vorschlag	fohrshlahg
suit *men*	der Anzug	antsoog
suit *women*	das Kostüm	kostuim
suitcase	der (Hand)koffer	(hant)koffer
summer	der Sommer	zommair
sun	die Sonne	zonner
sunbathe (to)	sonnenbaden	zonnen-bahden
sunburn	der Sonnenbrand	zonnen-brant
sunglasses	die Sonnenbrille	zonnen-briller
sunhat	der Sonnenhut	zonnen-hoot

sunny	**sonnig**	zonnikh
sunshade	**der Sonnenschirm**	zonnen-sheerm
suntan oil	**das Sonnenöl**	zonnen-erl
supper	**das Abendessen**	ahbent-essen
sure	**sicher**	zeekher
surfboard	**das Surfbrett**	serfbret
surgery	**das Sprechzimmer**	shprekh-tsimmer
surgery hours	**die Sprechstunde**	shprekh-stoonder
surprise	**die Überraschung**	uibair-rashoong
surprise (to)	**überraschen**	uibair-rashen
surroundings	**die Umgebung**	oomgayboong
suspender belt	**der Strumpfgürtel**	**shtroompf**-guirtel
sweater	**der Pullover**	poolohvair
sweet	**süss**	zuis
sweets	**die Bonbons**	bonbons
swell (to)	**anschwellen**	anshvellen
swim (to)	**schwimmen**	shvimmen
swimming pool	**die Badeanstalt**	bahder-anstalt
swings	**die Schaukel/die Wippe**	showkel/vipper
Swiss	**schweizerisch**	shvītserish
switch *elec.*	**der (Licht)schalter**	(likht)shaltair
Switzerland	**Schweiz**	shvīts
swollen	**angeschwollen**	angeshvollen
synagogue	**die Synagoge**	zuinagohger

T

table	der Tisch	tish
tablecloth	das Tischtuch	tishtookh
tablet	die Tablette	tabletter
tailor	der Schneider	shnīdair
take (to)	nehmen	naymen
talk (to)	reden	rayden
tall	gross	grohs
tampon	der Tampon	tampong
tank	der Tank	tank
tanned	sonnverbrannt	zonfairbrant
tap	der Wasserhahn	vassair-hahn
tapestry	der Wandteppich	vant-teppikh
taste	schmecken	shmecken
tax	die (Kur)taxe	(koor)-takser
taxi	das Taxi	taksee
taxi rank	der Taxistand	taksee-shtant
teach (to)	lehren	layren
tear	der Riss	ris
tear (to)	(zer)reissen	(tsair)rīssen
teaspoon	der Teelöffel	tay-lerffel
telegram	das Telegramm	taylegram
telephone	das Telefon	taylefohn
telephone (to)	telefonieren	taylefohneeren
telephone box	die Telefonzelle	taylefohn-tseller
telephone call	der Anruf	anroof

telephone directory	**das Telefonbuch**	taylefohn-bookh
telephone number	**die Telefonnummer**	taylefohn-noommair
telephone operator	**der Telefonist**	taylefohnist
telephone operator	**die Telefonistin**	taylefohnistin
television	**das Fernsehen**	fairnzayen
telex	**das Telex**	taylex
tell (to)	**erzählen**	airtsaylen
temperature	**die Temperatur**	tempairatoor
temple	**der Tempel**	tempel
temporary	**vorläufig/**	forloyfeekh/
	vorübergehend	foruibairgayent
tennis	**das Tennis**	tennis
tent	**das Zelt**	tselt
tent peg	**der Zeltpflock**	tselt-pflock
tent pole	**der Zeltmast**	tseltmast
terrace	**die Terrasse**	tairrasser
than	**als**	als
that	**jener/-e/-es**	yaynair/yayner/yaynes
the	**der/die/das**	dair/dee/das
theatre	**das Theater**	tayahtair
their(s)	**ihr/ihre**	eer/eerer
them	**sie/ihnen**	zee/eenen
then	**dann**	dan
there	**da/dort**	dah/dort
there is	**es ist/gibt**	es ist/geept
there are	**es sind/gibt**	es zint/geept

thermometer	das Thermometer	tairmohmaytair
these	diese	deezer
they	sie	zee
thick	dick	dick
thief	der Dieb	deep
thin	dünn	duin
thing	das Ding/die Sache	ding/zakher
think (to)	denken	denken
thirsty	durstig	doorstikh
this	dieser/-e/-es	deezair/deezer/deezes
those	jene	yayner
though	obwohl	opvohl
thread	der Faden	fahden
through	durch	doorkh
throughout	während	vairent
throw (to)	werfen	vairfen
thunder	der Donner	donnair
thunderstorm	das Gewitter	gevittair
ticket	die Karte	karter
ticket office	der Fahrkartenschalter	fahrkarten-shaltair
tide	die Gezeiten (pl.)	getsīten
tie	der Schlips	shlips
tie sport	der Gleichstand	glīkh-stant
tight	eng	eng
tights	die Strumpfhose	shtroompf-hohser

time	**die Zeit**	tsīt
timetable	**der Fahrplan**	fahrplahn
tin	**die Dose**	dohzer
tin opener	**der Dosenöffner**	dohzen-erfnair
tip	**das Trinkgeld**	trinkgelt
tip (to)	**ein Trinkgeld geben**	īn trinkgelt gayben
tired	**müde**	muider
tissues	**die Papiertücher**	papeer-tuikhair
to	**zu/nach**	tsoo/nahkh
tobacco	**der Tabak**	taback
tobacco pouch	**der Tabaksbeutel**	tabacksboytel
together	**zusammen**	tsoozammen
toilet	**die Toilette**	twaletter
toilet paper	**das Toilettenpapier**	twalettenpapeer
toll	**der Zoll**	tsoll
tomorrow	**morgen**	morgen
too *also*	**auch**	owkh
too (much, many)	**zu (viel/viele)**	tsoo (feel/feeler)
toothbrush	**die Zahnbürste**	tsahn-buirster
toothpaste	**die Zahnpasta**	tsahn-pasta
toothpick	**der Zahnstocher**	tsahn-shtokhair
top	**das obere Ende**	ohbairer ender
torch	**die Taschenlampe**	tashen-lamper
torn	**zerrissen**	tsairrissen
touch (to)	**berühren**	beruiren
tough	**hart/zäh**	hart/tsay

tour	die (Rund)reise	(roont)rīzer
tourist	der Tourist	tooreest
tourist office	das Fremdenverkehrs-büro	fremdenfairkayrs-buiroh
towards	gegen	gay-gen
towel	das Handtuch	hant-tookh
tower	der Turm	toorm
town	die Stadt	shtat
town hall	das Rathaus	rahthows
toy	das Spielzeug	shpeel-tsoyg
traffic	der Verkehr	fairkayr
traffic jam	die Verkehrsstockung	fairkayrs-shtockoong
traffic lights	die Verkehrsampel	fairkairs-ampel
trailer	der Anhänger	anhenger
train	der Zug	tsoog
tram	die Strassenbahn	shtrahssenbahn
transfer (to)	übertragen	uibertrahgen
transfer (to) *travel*	umbuchen	oombookhen
transit	der Durchgang	doorkhgang
translate (to)	übersetzen	uiber-zetsen
travel (to)	reisen	rīzen
travel agency	das Reisebüro	rīzer-buiroh
traveller	der Reisende	rīzender
travellers' cheque	der Reisescheck	rīzer-sheck
treat (to)	behandeln	behandeln

treatment	die Behandlung	behantloong
tree	der Baum	bowm
trip	der Ausflug	owsfloog
trouble	die Mühe	mui-er
trousers	die Hose *sing.*	hohzer
true	wahr	vahr
trunk	der Koffer	koffair
trunks *swimming*	die Badehose	bahder-hohzer
truth	die Wahrheit	vahrhīt
try (to)	versuchen	fairzookhen
try on (to)	anprobieren	anprohbeeren
tunnel	der Tunnel	toon-nel
turn (to)	umdrehen	oomdrayen
turning	die Biegung	beegoong
tweezers	die Pinzette *sing.*	pintsetter
twin-bedded room	das Zweibettzimmer	tsvībet-tsimmer
twisted	verrenkt	fairrenkt
typewriter	die Schreibmaschine	shrīb-masheener

U

ugly	hässlich	heslikh
umbrella	der Regenschirm	raygensheerm
(beach) umbrella	der (Sonnen)schirm	(zonnen)sheerm
uncle	der Onkel	onkel
uncomfortable	unbequem	oonbekvaym
unconscious	bewusstlos	bevoost-lohs

under(neath)	unter	oontair
underground	die U-Bahn	oo-bahn
understand (to)	verstehen	fairshtayen
underwater fishing	die Unterwasser-fischerei	oontairvasser-fisherī
underwear	die Unterwäsche	oontair-vesher
university	die Universität	ooneevairseetayt
unpack (to)	auspacken	owspacken
until	bis	bis
unusual	ungewöhnlich	oongevernlikh
up	auf	owf
upstairs	oben	ohben
urgent	dringend	dringent
us	uns	oons
USA	die Vereinigten Staaten	fairīnigten shtahten
use (to)	brauchen	browkhen
useful	brauchbar	browkhbahr
useless	unbrauchbar	oonbrowkhbahr
usual	gewöhnlich	gevernlikh

V

vacancies	Zimmer frei	tsimmer frī
vacant	frei	frī
vacation	die Ferien	faireeyen
valid	gültig	guiltikh

valley	**das Tal**	tahl
valuable	**wertvoll**	vairtfol
value	**der Wert**	vairt
vase	**die Vase**	vahzer
VAT	**die Mehrwertsteuer**	mayrvayrt-shtoyair
vegetable	**das Gemüse**	gemuizer
vegetarian	**der Vegetarier**	fegetahree-air
vein	**die Ader**	ahdair
velvet	**der Samt**	zamt
ventilation	**die Ventilation**	ventilahtsyohn
very	**sehr**	zayr
very much	**viel/sehr**	feel/zayr
vest	**das Unterhemd**	oontairhemt
video cassette	**die Videokassette**	veedayoh-kassetter
video recorder	**der Video-Recorder**	veedayoh-raykordair
view	**der Blick**	blik
villa	**die Villa**	veelah
village	**das Dorf**	dorf
vineyard	**der Weinberg**	vīnbairg
violin	**die Geige**	gīger
visa	**das Visum**	veezoom
visibility	**die Sicht(barkeit)**	sikhtbahrkīt
visit	**der Besuch**	bezookh
visit (to)	**besuchen**	bezookhen
voice	**die Stimme**	shtimmer
voltage	**die Spannung**	shpannoong

| voucher | der Gutschein | gootshīn |
| voyage | die Reise | rīzer |

V

wait (to)	warten	varten
waiter	der Kellner	kelnair
waiting room	der Warteraum	varter-rowm
waitress	die Kellnerin	kelnerin
wake (to)	aufwachen	owf-vakhen
Wales	Wales	vayls
walk	der Spaziergang	shpatseer-gang
walk (to)	spazierengehen	shpatseeren-gayen
wall inside	die Wand	vant
wall outside	die Mauer	mowair
wall plug	der Stecker	shteckair
wallet	die Brieftasche	breef-tasher
want (to)	wollen	vollen
wardrobe	der Kleiderschrank	klīder-shrank
warm	warm	varm
wash (to)	waschen	vashen
washbasin	das Waschbecken	vash-becken
waste	der Abfall	apfal
waste (to)	verschwenden	fairshvenden
watch	die Armbanduhr	armbant-oor
water	das Wasser	vassair
waterfall	der Wasserfall	vassairful

waterproof	**wasserdicht**	vassairdikht
water skiing	**das Wasserskilaufen**	vassair-shee-lowfen
wave	**die Welle**	veller
way	**der Weg**	vayg
we	**wir**	veer
wear (to)	**tragen**	trahgen
weather	**das Wetter**	vetter
weather forecast	**die Wettervorhersage/ der Wetterbericht**	vettair-fohrhayr-zahger/ vettairberikht
wedding ring	**der Ehering**	ay-ering
week	**die Woche**	vokher
weigh (to)	**wiegen**	veegen
weight	**das Gewicht**	gevikht
welcome	**willkommen**	vilkommen
well	**gut**	goot
well *water*	**der Brunnen**	broonen
Welsh	**walisisch**	valeezish
west	**der Westen**	vesten
wet	**nass**	nas
what?	**was?**	vas
wheel	**das Rad**	raht
wheelchair	**der Rollstuhl**	rollshtool
when?	**wann?**	van
where?	**wo?**	voh
whether	**ob**	op

which?	welcher/-e/-es?	velkhair/velkher/velkhes
while	während	vairent
who?	wer?	vair
whole	ganz	gants
whose?	wessen?	vessen
why?	warum?	vahroom
wide	weit	vīt
widow	die Witwe	veetver
widower	der Witwer	veetvair
wife	die Frau	frow
wild	wild	vilt
win (to)	gewinnen	gevinnen
wind	der Wind	vint
window	das Fenster	fenstair
wine merchant	der Weinhändler	vīn-hendlair
wing	der Flügel	fluigel
winter	der Winter	vintair
winter sports	der Wintersport	vintair-shport
wire	der Draht	draht
wish (to)	wünschen	vuinshen
with	mit	mit
without	ohne	ohner
woman	die Frau	frow
wonderful	wundervoll	voondair-foll
wood	der Wald	valt
wood *timber*	das Holz	holts

wool	**die Wolle**	voller
word	**das Wort**	vort
work	**die Arbeit**	arbīt
work (to)	**arbeiten**	arbīten
worry (to)	**(sich) beunruhigen**	(zikh) beoonroo-eegen
worse	**schlechter**	shlekhtair
worth (to be)	**wert sein**	vairt zīn
wrap (to)	**wickeln**	vickeln
write (to)	**schreiben**	shrīben
writing paper	**das Schreibpapier**	shrīp-papeer
wrong	**falsch**	falsh

X

| xerox | **die Xerocopie** | ksayroh-kohpee |
| X-ray | **die Röntgenaufnahme** | rerntgen-owfnahmer |

Y

yacht	**die Jacht**	yakht
year	**das Jahr**	yahr
yesterday	**gestern**	gestairn
yet	**noch**	nokh
you	**Sie/du** (*familiar*)	zee/doo
young	**jung**	yoong
your	**Ihr/dein**	eer/dīn
youth hostel	**die Jugendherberge**	yoogent-hair-bairger

Z

| zip | der Reissverschluss | rīs-fairshlooss |
| zoo | der Zoo | tsoh |

INDEX